# A.M. NAIK

## Advance Praise

A.M. Naik is among those rare people who combine vision and execution. His deep sense of patriotism and his keen intellect, combined, have enabled him to pursue relentlessly the mission of establishing India as a global leader in the manufacturing arena. Naik is an amazing leader who can conceive bold ideas, transmit his passion to his team and then provide the leadership to realize them. His legendary people skills are very well known. He always had the courage and conviction to chart a new course of vision for his organization, one that combined the hallowed traditions of the enterprise with an entrepreneurial zeal, a nationalistic fervour and a strong emphasis on wealth-creation. It is this new avatar of L&T that most of us are familiar with today. The phenomenal journey of Naik captured in this book reinforces the age-old principle that in life, as in business, it doesn't matter who you are or where you hail from. Your ability to excel in a chosen endeavour is determined solely by the path you have set for yourself. I am sure the youth of India, especially the budding entrepreneurs who are in the business of building lasting legacies, will have a lot to learn and gain inspiration from A.M. Naik and this book.

—**Mukesh Ambani**
Chairman and managing director, Reliance Industries

Anil Manibhai Naik is an exceptional individual, whom I have had the pleasure of meeting on several occasions over the last three decades. A true nation-builder, he built an industry, equivalent to the best in the world, and has done so much for the country.

Also, beyond his professional achievements, he has consistently shown a deep devotion to the community. It was a few years ago when Apollo had the opportunity to collaborate with the hospitals set up by his trust in Navsari, Gujarat. What I had previously only heard about became evident before my eyes: Naik is undoubtedly one of the world's most outstanding business leaders. His unwavering dedication and entrepreneurial spirit transformed L&T into a unique global organization. Furthermore, as a philanthropist, his inspiring decision to establish hospitals in his birthplace to serve the community sets a remarkable example for young leaders to follow. Hopefully, with more business leaders participating in healthcare, we can gradually alleviate the shortage of health infrastructure in India.

**—Dr Prathap C. Reddy**
Founder-chairman, Apollo Hospitals

The best of professionals are focused on adding value through all their efforts. Clearly, A.M. Naik is an excellent example of such a professional.

Throughout his career, Naik has tried his best to add value to everything he has undertaken—leading a business, working with the government and engaging with people and societal issues.

I have known him for years, and his dynamic and energetic leadership has always impressed me. He was significantly responsible for creating L&T's IT business, which is now counted in the top bracket of the industry. This book is a must-read for those who want to learn from his rich experiences.

**—Azim Premji**
Founder-chairman, Wipro

Few people carry the flag of India Inc. as proudly as Mr A.M. Naik does. He can be aggressive, even combative, in defending the interests of his country and of the company of which he is at the helm. All of us in industry and business know that Naik's heart is in the right place. I have known him for decades now, and our interactions have always been stimulating because he is restless with the status quo. He is bursting with creative energy and always wants to do something different. For those who may not know him so well, this biography gives a peek into his life and the remarkable work that he has done.

—**Deepak Parekh**
Former chairman, HDFC

Naik is more than a doyen of the industry. He is a multidimensional personality whom the Sanskrit description 'ashtavadhani' fits. A natural-born leader, he is a rare visionary with a towering engineering mind and matching commercial expertise. Endowed with a matchless brain-and-brawn combination that challenged his age, he understands law, accounts, finance and economics like any domain expert. A compassionate philanthropist, Naik's staunch nationalism crowns his strong personality. This book presents his full self.

—**S. Gurumurthy**
Writer, journalist and corporate advisor

Having served on the board of Larsen & Toubro and as a banker to the group, I am a first-hand admirer of the many facets of Naik—from the astute, hard-driving business leader, to the gutsy entrepreneur, to—increasingly now—a committed and outcome-oriented philanthropist. There is a lot to learn from his zestful, never-say-die approach to life.

—**Naina Lal Kidwai**
Chairperson, Rothschild & Co

# A.M. NAIK

## THE MAN WHO BUILT TOMORROW

### PRIYA KUMAR
### JAIRAM N. MENON

HARPER
BUSINESS

*An Imprint of* HarperCollins *Publishers*

First published in India by Harper Business
An imprint of HarperCollins *Publishers* 2024
4th Floor, Tower A, Building No. 10, DLF Cyber City,
DLF Phase II, Gurugram, Haryana – 122002
www.harpercollins.co.in

2 4 6 8 10 9 7 5 3 1

Copyright © Priya Kumar and Jairam N. Menon 2024

P-ISBN: 978-93-5699-747-9
E-ISBN: 978-93-5699-692-2

The views and opinions expressed in this book are the authors' own and the facts are as reported by them, and the publishers are not in any way liable for the same.

Priya Kumar and Jairam N. Menon assert the moral right to be identified as the authors of this work.

All rights reserved. No part of this publication may be reproduced, stored in a retrieval system, or transmitted, in any form or by any means, electronic, mechanical, photocopying, recording or otherwise, without the prior permission of the publishers.

Typeset in 12/17.4 Baskerville at
Manipal Technologies Limited, Manipal

Printed and bound at
Thomson Press (India) Ltd

This book is produced from independently certified FSC® paper
to ensure responsible forest management.

*To all those who steadfastly hold the spirit of nationalism, entrepreneurship, personal accountability and concern for the public good over and beyond their roles, responsibilities and titles.*

# Contents

| | | |
|---|---|---|
| | *Authors' Note* | xi |
| | *Foreword* | xiii |
| | *Prelude* | xvii |
| 1. | Game On! | 1 |
| 2. | Hazira: From Marshland to Mega Engineering Complex | 17 |
| 3. | One Battle, Many Victories | 33 |
| 4. | The New L&T | 45 |
| 5. | India First, India Always | 71 |
| 6. | IT: A Vision Vindicated | 95 |
| 7. | Building Relationships That Last | 107 |
| 8. | Building Tomorrow's People | 117 |

## Contents

| | | |
|---|---|---|
| 9. | What Sets Naik Apart | 141 |
| 10. | Family: Pillars of Support | 157 |
| 11. | Giving Back, the Naik Way | 175 |
| 12. | The Flag Flies High | 201 |
| | *Acknowledgements* | 221 |

# Authors' Note

TWO VOYAGERS FROM DISTINCT VOCATIONS CAME TOGETHER, entrusted with a difficult mission—to build the narrative of the man who is building tomorrow. But, we said, the story of A.M. Naik has been told before, and most people know it already. Never mind, we were informed; there is more to say.

We soon realized there will always be more to say, because the man at the centre of it all will not stand still. Indeed, he cannot stand still. Uncertain but excited, we ventured into the many worlds that Naik inhabits—nation-building, industry, mentoring leaders and the expanding universe of philanthropy.

After writing this book, we do know much more than we knew before, but we are nowhere near complete. We are artists who have painted a few brush strokes here, etched details there and cast new light where we could. Does all this add up to a whole new

## Authors' Note

portrait? Yes and no. Yes, because we have put in details elicited from the interviews we conducted with over sixty people spread across geographies. And no, because Naik is a man who is building tomorrow, and tomorrow is always a moving target. There can be no full stops to Naik's achievements.

If there are errors or omissions in our narrative, we take responsibility. The subject is too vast, varied and constantly evolving, and we were left feeling our way. If we have managed to reflect Naik's extraordinary life and times with a fair degree of accuracy, we credit the accomplishment to all those people who gave so freely of their time in helping us put this volume together. The narrative in the following pages is not in our voice alone; it is a medley of many; and the portrait we set out to sketch is a mosaic. Put it all together, and you will glimpse A.M. Naik, chairman emeritus of Larsen & Toubro, nationalist and philanthropist.

# Foreword

ALL BUSINESS LEADERS WEAR THEIR CORPORATES ON THEIR SLEEVE. But A.M. Naik—rising from the shop floor of Larsen & Toubro to occupy its topmost post, propelling it into a global giant and a strategic national asset—wears India on his sleeve.

Naik was in business, but he was not just a businessman. He was a CEO but not *just* a CEO. He was neither the owner nor the promoter of L&T, but he owned and promoted it. He made close to one-sixth of L&T's ownership vest in its employees, by way of an innovative and outstanding court-approved demerger plan. Besides making L&T a majorly employee-owned firm, the plan ring-fenced it from hostile takeover bids by private interests that had earlier threatened it, twice. With that strategic move, he not only released its entrepreneurial spirit that professionally managed companies are

## Foreword

said to miss but also vested in it a semi-public character, enabling it to partner governments with moral ease.

What marked him out as a corporate leader was his vision for L&T, which was integral to his vision for India. That manifested in the rise of L&T as a strategic partner in areas of national defence and security. His business life is, of course, a tale of corporate prowess, success, turnover, profits and market cap. L&T excelled in every test and outperformed its peers and others. His corporate career is a testament to the blend of foresight and insight. His leadership of L&T and the Indian industry was recognized and celebrated by business associations, the media and society. The greatest of recognitions came to him from the government, which decorated him with the second-highest national honour, the Padma Vibhushan.

In a rising India, businesses and corporates are as integral as education and public or social services—not in competition or conflict with them. Wrong notions of business and government relations have damaged both in the past. Just as the period before the 1990s demonstrated that control of business was wrong, the swing to the other extreme proved that unregulated business is as dangerous. A fair regulation aided by mutual trust and understanding between business and government is sine qua non for businesses and the economy. Mutual trust has to be founded on national and public interest as the common value towering over everything. Here, the rise of L&T may have some valuable lessons for Indian corporates.

The late autumn of Naik's life comes in the second part of his biography. This will complete the narrative of his corporate journey, which ends with the handing over of the L&T flag to

## Foreword

the successor he has selected with forensic care to head and run the illustrious company. Naik's biography and the L&T story are almost inseparable as he had virtually no life or interest outside L&T. Naik's journey as the leader of a corporate with a semi-public character will have this profound message for young Indians in business and corporates, as India marches towards becoming the world's third-largest economy and a developed nation by 2047—a journey and goal set by the prime minister for the Azadi Amrit Kaal.

A nationalist to the core, Naik's life of commitment to the nation and society is incomplete without mentioning his huge philanthropy. Born to a humble schoolteacher in a village, he donated the largest part of the wealth he generated, always by the right means, for public good—a moral lesson from Naik for all those who build wealth through high-yielding business and corporate mechanisms.

**Ajit Doval**
National Security Advisor

# Prelude

In a high-domed hall of New Delhi's Rashtrapati Bhavan, the large, distinguished gathering is hushed in anticipation. Above the muted buzz, the voice of the announcer comes through like a clarion: 'Shri Anilkumar Manibhai Naik, vyapar evam udyog [business and industry].' A cheer goes up, and applause rises to a crescendo as Naik gets up and takes measured steps towards the podium.

The hall has played host to epochal moments in India's history, and is doing so again for the investiture of India's national awards on a sunny Saturday in March 2019. As he walks along the carpet, Naik passes some of the country's most distinguished citizens, including the prime minister and senior members of his cabinet. He nods to the faces he recognizes, and then turns to greet the President of India, Shri Ram Nath Kovind, with a namaste.

# Prelude

The President places a medallion on Naik's chest—the coveted Padma Vibhushan. Bronze-coloured and ornately engraved, it is a disk that exudes gravitas. Embossed at its centre is the lotus, India's national flower, a peerless symbol of the beauty of accomplishment. The President also hands over a large ceremonial scroll, wound into an elegant cylinder. Bowing deeply, Naik turns and walks back, applause accompanying his steps all the way.

The Padma Vibhushan, India's second-highest civilian award, is the nation's public recognition of the efforts of its finest citizens. The citation says it is being given for 'exceptional and distinguished service'. Few people have received such honour in the nearly seven-decade history of the Padma awards. Even fewer—in fact, just twelve—have received the honour while serving industry as corporate professionals. Naik belongs to this rare category. He heads an organization whose course and character, profile and pace, he has reshaped. Larsen & Toubro, or L&T, is no ordinary company; it is widely recognized as a nation-builder, moulding the India of the twenty-first century. Equally, the Padma Vibhushan is a recognition of Naik's expansive, outcome-oriented philanthropy, which is making a difference to thousands of lives in Mumbai and south Gujarat.

Sitting back in his chair, Naik glances at the medallion and certificate, and pauses to reflect on his life. What an extraordinary journey it has been, from the hinterland of south Gujarat, step by step, to the top echelons of corporate India.

When he speaks about this journey, it's more than a historical narrative of stellar accomplishment; it is a road map to realizing

## Prelude

one's aspirations. The inner aspects of this journey are also very significant.

In the following pages, you will travel with Naik through a recap of that long journey. It's a lesson in how the present can be leveraged to shape a new destiny, a new tomorrow. It is inspiring, exhilarating and, ultimately, deeply fulfilling.

### *A.M. Naik's Padma Vibhushan Acceptance Speech*

I have always considered myself fortunate to be in a position of service to India and millions of my fellow countrymen. To secure high national honour for such service is a matter of the utmost joy. For me, the Padma Vibhushan is also an acknowledgement of the contribution made to nation, industry and society by Larsen & Toubro—the company I am proud to have served for over five decades, and led for the last two. I thank the Government of India for this honour, and use this opportunity to congratulate my fellow awardees, who have won recognition in different fields.

# 1

## Game On!

*'My dream career has always been one that would give me the opportunity to participate in the grand mission of building the nation.'*

A.M. NAIK'S FIRST JOB INTERVIEW AT LARSEN & TOUBRO IS NOW part of corporate legend. It's a story that has been told and re-told, excerpted and featured in books. It's more than the usual interplay of an eager aspirant and a large organization, more than the mishaps often caused in translation. This story is really all about the striking characteristics of a confident, young candidate who knew his mind, could take the rough with the smooth and was resolved that he would never give up on his dream.

It was November 1964 when Naik, a twenty-two-year-old engineering graduate, chanced upon a recruitment advertisement for L&T. He quickly read through the job description, requisite qualifications and experience, and felt reasonably confident that he ticked all the boxes. Things fell in place, and soon he found himself outside the cabin of a workshop foreman named T. Baker.

He had been forewarned. A neighbour who worked for L&T had cautioned him the previous evening that the foreman was known to be very tough: 'That T in his name stands for "terror". I wish you luck.'

As he waited on an old cane-backed chair outside Baker's cabin, young Naik sensed that this was a moment of destiny. He had been hearing of L&T since his college days. It had been on his radar as one of the companies that would meet his twin criteria for a career—one that would bring his engineering skills to the fore and, equally importantly, would in some way help participate in the grand task of building the nation. At L&T, both his criteria converged.

Here he was, at the doorway to his dream. Was he nervous? Unlikely. If you know A.M. Naik, nervousness is not one of his characteristics. He waited calmly until he was called in. After the briefest of pleasantries came the technical nitty-gritty.

And then, the make-or-break question: 'Do you know how to design a boiler?' Naik knew the answer well—as it turned out, better than the interviewer. Rather than plunging headfirst into the answer, Naik asked for details—thin cylinder or thick, size, material—and other questions that revealed his command over the subject. The terror had been tamed and Baker was impressed with the young man's grasp of the minutiae of engineering. Soon, the terms of employment were discussed and agreed upon.

## Game On!

'I am through,' the elated Naik must have told himself. But there was a hitch.

'You will also have to meet the old man,' said Baker, almost as an afterthought.

'Old man' was informal British slang that Naik did not quite catch. As it turned out, this was the sharp, keen-eyed engineer Gunnar Hansen. In contrast to the loud and gruff Baker, Hansen was cold and unsmiling; where Baker spoke English with an Aberdeen flavour, Hansen expressed himself in a Nordic drawl.

Today, decades later, Naik can still imitate the musical rhythm of Hansen's speech with surprising accuracy.

'How many people report to you?' Hansen asked.

'About three hundred and fifty,' Naik replied.

Hansen appeared surprised. 'That's a lot! Three hundred and fifty is a lot. It will be a *looong* time before you get that kind of responsibility at Larsen & Toubro,' he exclaimed.

Naik had still not come to grips with the English language—he would translate the question into his native Gujarati, think up an answer and translate it back into English. In the days to come, he would work assiduously on improving his linguistic abilities—listening to audio cassettes for hours to improve his diction and practising diligently before a mirror till he got the gestures and expressions right. He would become adept at holding large audiences in corporate and business meetings riveted with his eloquence. But at that moment, sitting before Hansen, he followed his usual drill—English to Gujarati (question), Gujarati to English (answer).

Out came the reply: 'Who knows, time will tell.'

## A.M. Naik

Now, that doesn't sound offensive in Gujarati, but to Hansen's ears it seemed like a cocky boast. He peremptorily told Naik to leave the room. End of interview. Had Naik's dream ended before it began?

In a couple of minutes, Baker also hurried out of the room, clearly upset with the way things had turned out. As he stomped down the corridor, the Scottish foreman, always liberal with his expletives, was heard mumbling and muttering: 'This is **** terrible. Why can't they just allow me to take the people I **** need? The company will miss a good catch.' The rant continued all the way up the stairs.

Finally, in his cabin, he turned to Naik and broke the news—Hansen thought he was overconfident, so all the terms Naik and Baker had agreed upon had been revised downwards. Baker spelt out the new offer—junior engineer instead of assistant engineer, ₹670 per month instead of ₹760, appointment in the 'unionized' category, not the 'supervisory' cadre.

Everything had gone south, but Naik's dreams were—and are—made of sterner stuff. He turned to Baker and said: 'Don't worry, Mr Baker. It was my dream to join L&T, and I am going to join anyway.'

This was music to Baker's ears, and the old warhorse offered parting words of reassurance.

'My sonny boy, work hard, work hard,' he said. 'And on confirmation, we will give you back all that we had promised.'

Work hard Naik did. An era had begun.

# Game On!

## '... I have recruited forty-one engineers and sacked thirty-eight. I don't want you to be the thirty-ninth.'

On Naik's first day at L&T, Baker told him: 'Since 1958, I've recruited forty-one engineers and sacked thirty-eight. I don't want you to be the thirty-ninth.'

Not the most propitious way to greet a fresh employee, but that was Baker's gruff style of conditioning a newcomer. That would have psyched out most newcomers, but to Naik, it sounded like the rousing notes of a bugle—it was a call to battle, and he relished such challenges. Game on!

Naik put in long hours not because Baker had told him to or because this was his dream career destination and he had to make a good impression. He worked hard because that is the only way he knows. Even in the company where he had been previously employed, a small Parsi-owned firm called Nestor Boilers, Naik had very quickly caught the eye of the bosses. In fact, he had been marked out for an early promotion and deputation to the United Kingdom for international exposure.

Why did he want to jettison those promising prospects and look for a new position at L&T? The reason is not something you normally come across with someone at the start of his career—it was a matter of principle, the likes of which would go on to shape the course of his career at crucial junctures.

Naik had overheard a senior colleague being publicly berated by the son of the proprietor of Nestor Boilers. Naik did not catch what exactly had transpired, but he distinctly heard the elderly engineer being told: 'I pay you ₹750 for the work you do. I can get it done for ₹250.'

The incident disturbed Naik. He asked himself the question he inevitably ends up asking when faced with a dilemma: would his father have approved of a boss talking to an employee like this? The answer stared him in the face, and so, the star employee of Nestor Boilers decided to look for a new job.

They say destiny cannot be denied; at best, it can be deferred. Naik had not been able to join the company he had set his sights on right after graduating, because in those days, L&T only took in IIT graduates, and he was from Birla Vishvakarma Mahavidyalaya in Anand, Gujarat. But now, here he was, inside L&T's cavernous workshop, poised to build a new tomorrow, and many tomorrows thereafter.

---

Naik threw himself wholeheartedly into his role. Far from giving Baker cause to be the thirty-ninth engineer to be summarily dismissed, he achieved distinction by being the one to break the mould in many ways. Conventionally, supervisors are expected to sit in their air-conditioned offices and, well, 'supervise'. Naik was a doer; he loved to be where the action was, preferring the sweat and grime of the shop floor. He was rarely at his desk—a fact that alarmed Baker because he thought his 'sonny boy' was playing hooky. When told about Naik's hands-on style, he is said to have nodded in appreciation, mumbling: 'Good man, good man.'

## Game On!

In workshops around the world, there is no love lost between engineers and non-engineering professionals. The technicians are convinced that the engineers are a pampered lot who can only spout the theoretical knowledge they acquired in college, while they, the technicians, do all the real work. Baker himself had risen from being a copper welder, and he naturally looked with disdain at engineers. 'Bloody **** engineers sitting on their ****, telling me how a boiler should be made!'

But everyone acknowledged that Naik was different—an engineer who had his feet on the ground and did not mind getting his hands smeared with grease. An engineer, in fact, after Baker's own heart. When Naik was confirmed in service, Baker did what he said he would. He 'fought with the old man' to restore Naik's salary to ₹760 and make him an assistant engineer. Then, he fought some more to pave the way for more promotions. Naik would soon get ₹950 per month, eventually reaching ₹1,125. Yet, there was not a man around who would grudge him his rapid rise—he had earned every rupee of it.

Baker is no more, but we had a phone call with Naik's former boss, M.H. Pherwani, who is now in the United States. Pherwani, a gold medallist in college, is described in the 'history' section of L&T's Experience Centre in Powai as being 'incandescently brilliant'. He had risen to become a director on the L&T board when he decided to quit and pursue a career with the World Bank. Now happily retired, Pherwani recalled the days when a young Naik was part of his team at L&T's workshops.

'Naik is like a tearaway thoroughbred horse. You could bet a million dollars on Naik, and you'd be guaranteed not only a victory but also some record-breaking feats along the way,' Pherwani said.

'Watching him work could sometimes exhaust the observer. I'd advise him to take a break, but he was always on his feet. His calendar and plans were scheduled by the hour, the minute. Keeping up with him wasn't just hard—it was impossible.'

---

One of Naik's former comrades-in-arms who looks upon him as an 'elder brother' is the tall, dapper K. Venkataramanan, called 'KV' by almost everyone across L&T. When we went to meet him at his home, perched high on a beachfront tower, KV had just returned from a vigorous game of badminton, or perhaps tennis or golf or cricket—he is adept at them all. A product of IIT, he is everything you would expect a top-flight professional to be—brilliant engineer, sparkling conversationalist and cued in to the latest in any field you can think of. Naik and KV go back a long way, to their days together on the shop floor in Powai. When the two converse, it seems like old troopers reminiscing about their victorious campaigns.

KV describes Naik as a fountain from which you can 'imbibe good qualities'. But, he cautions, you need to be selective. 'Many people tried to copy him, but none of them made it to the greatness that he did. You cannot be Tendulkar; you cannot be Kishore Kumar. So, what I did was pick up the qualities I could assimilate. He has so many good qualities that it is easy to pick those most suitable to your disposition. You can be parts of him, but never the whole,' KV says.

Guru and shishya bonded well, and the association they formed continues to be as robust as ever, as Naik forged high-trajectory career paths for them.

## Seeking diversity

Among the many fresh concepts Naik brought centre stage was the importance of demographic diversity. The term 'DE&I', which stands for diversity, equity and inclusion, may be trendy now, with woke human resource departments clamouring for it in increasingly strident tones. But Naik had encountered the lack of DE&I nearly six decades ago. In fact, of all the problems that he overcame in the early part of his career, this was the most intriguing.

A decade earlier, L&T had set up one of industry's first Apprentice Training Schemes to provide a steady stream of trained manpower to the workshops. It worked like a charm initially, and L&T-trained apprentices were much sought-after in industry. But the scheme was vitiated when parochialism raised its unseemly head. Even a casual observer could note that all the apprentices who cleared the entrance tests happened to hail from a single region of the country. Candidates from Maharashtra, where the facility is located, did not get a look-in at all.

This had ominous political ramifications. It wasn't long before the issue was taken up by Balasaheb Thackeray, the charismatic political leader who shot to prominence by eloquently espousing the cause of local populace. He rang up L&T's co-founder Henning

Holck-Larsen and politely asked for the matter to be looked into. At that time, Thackeray had the city in thrall, and his complaint sent tremors down the company—right from Holck-Larsen through Gunnar Hansen to Baker. All of them acknowledged the problem, but none of them could fathom the reason behind it. At first glance, all the procedures and rules were seemingly followed dutifully, and Baker studiously maintained his rigorous and impartial interview routine. Still, the results were much the same as before—candidates from outside the state were sweeping all the vacancies on offer. Soon enough, another call—less polite than before—came from Thackeray to Holck-Larsen.

This time, the hot potato was tossed to Naik—the troubleshooter for all seasons. With his earthy, practical wisdom, Naik quickly figured out how the system was being gamed. Applications from smart local candidates were being held back. Only the dregs were sent to Baker who promptly shot them down. Naik had the answer. He had an advertisement released in mainstream newspapers and assigned a trustworthy assistant to handle all the applications received, process them and ensure that they reached Baker's in-tray. The results were obvious within a month. The demographic balance was restored as a crop of local candidates with impeccable credentials joined the workforce; Holck-Larsen received no more calls from Balasaheb Thackeray.

To say that Baker was relieved would be an understatement. Naik had proved that he could crack a problem that had foxed the rest for long. More importantly, he cemented his reputation for being firm but fair. This was to prove valuable when he confronted the sterner challenges ahead.

# Game On!

Not even an ounce of parochialism has ever tainted Naik's mind—his single-minded, almost manic, obsession with merit left no room for any other consideration. Even a quick look at the company's history tells us that those closest to him across his working life were people from across the country.

## 'Will there be trouble?'

Naik heard the anxiety in the voice of the top-level L&T executive on the other end of the phone: 'Will there be trouble in Powai?' There was also perhaps a hint of apprehension because in those days, corporate management was based at L&T House in Ballard Estate, thirty kilometres from Powai, and had no way of gauging the situation on the shop floor.

Naik's response was measured and balanced: 'Ninety-nine per cent there should be no trouble. If there *is* trouble, we will have to deal with it.'

The answer had everything from a candid appraisal of the risks involved and, an understanding of the situation to an unostentatious but emphatic demonstration of courage. Slowly, almost inevitably, because of all that he had done, Naik had become the only person from the management who could feel the pulse of the workers. He was not only the barometer of mood and temperature but also the best man to handle a crisis if matters got out of hand.

One of the persons close to Naik, then and now, is V. K. Magapu, a star graduate of IIT Madras. Now leading a comfortably retired life in Pune, Magapu came to meet us in Mumbai. He told us that Naik was the only person who knew how to tackle the union, and he did it while adopting 'a collaborative approach'. This is something not many in industry could emulate successfully.

Labour trouble had been the bane of Indian industry from the 1960s through the 1980s. Organized labour was propped up by unions affiliated to political parties. These unions would call for a strike whenever they felt aggrieved, and they could feel aggrieved for the flimsiest of reasons—a request, for instance, that they refrain from sleeping on duty. When faced with this volatile situation, managers and supervisors could take one of two routes—play the populist boss by allowing the workers a free hand or crack the whip and ignore the consequences. In between these extremes lay a thin line, which Naik walked.

He was tough—very tough—when required because 'rules were rules' and discipline could not be compromised. The night shift was one that traditionally saw a precipitous drop in productivity; workers would tend to nod off, and the more enterprising ones even ventured out to the nearby Powai Lake and tried their hand at angling. On the occasions that they were lucky, the dinner menu would have a welcome addition!

All this had been going on for a while, and most supervisors and managers had thought it prudent to look away.

They would tell each other, in cynical resignation: 'What can be done? The union is too powerful.' But Naik put a stop to it—no more freelance fishing.

Despite this 'tough boss' image, he could be understanding and considerate too. He knew most of the workers by name, knew their families. When they needed help, he was the one they turned to.

## Game On!

In walking this tightrope, fear of personal safety was something that did not enter his calculations. He had not backed down when confronted with bullies during college elections, and he did not feel intimidated by belligerent labour unions.

Perhaps, he recollected the line his father had told him: 'If you have done nothing wrong, you have no reason to fear.'

As years passed, Naik struck up an excellent rapport with Balasaheb Thackeray. In a world where leaders pussyfooted around critical issues, both Thackeray and Naik recognized each other as straight-talkers, unafraid to speak their mind. When Thackeray passed away in 2012, Naik wrote a condolence piece for L&T's in-house magazine.

'I have had the good fortune of interacting with him on several occasions. His fighting spirit, unmatched oratory skills and versatility in several fields made my interactions with him memorable for life,' he wrote.

'Balasaheb has always been very appreciative of the work our company did, and we shared similar views on several key issues. He always appreciated L&T's role in nation-building. Due to his vision and encouragement, our union worked in a constructive spirit with the management, and aligned itself with our company's larger goals.'

Three years later, in 2015, Balasaheb's son Uddhav Thackeray would be the guest of honour at a function held in Powai, to honour Naik on completing fifty years of service.

'I have not come here for a corporate function. I have come here because I consider Naik saheb's fifty-year milestone as a happy event in my family,' Uddhav told the gathering.

# A.M. Naik

## Working harder during a career plateau

It would be untrue to claim that Naik's early career was one long, heady swoosh of success. Yes, the rise in the early years had been meteoric, with the increasing compensation reflecting the pace of his growth. But Naik grew so rapidly that he overshot the norms set by the HR department. The trailblazer was deemed too young to take on any more responsibilities. The HR heads seemed to be saying 'spare a thought' for Naik's counterparts in other departments, whom he would have left far behind.

This would have led to the phenomenon of 'averaging of excellence' that compels organizations to treat star performers on par with the rest. Naik encountered a career plateau around 1974, facing a promotion drought that lasted over six years after reaching the position of general manager. True to his nature, during this phase, Naik worked harder than ever. As Martin Luther King Jr said in a different context, 'We must accept finite disappointment, but never lose infinite hope.' Naik firmly believed that both he and the company he had chosen would eventually do well.

In fact, so many of Naik's actions as a working professional were born out of the sterling values he learnt as a child. So many of his character traits are based on watching his father and grandfather as they went about their work, while some come from an inborn sense of mischief.

We will begin with the mischief. Young Anil was an incorrigible prankster, the cause of much mayhem in the neighbourhood. All the high-spirited misdeeds would be reported to his mother, who, in turn, narrated them verbatim to his schoolteacher father. After a cautionary word to young Anil, his father would take his mother aside and cheer her up with homespun philosophy: 'Only mischievous children achieve something in life.'

Mischievous or not, Naik achieved a lot in his professional career, and this was just the beginning. Legend tells us that Alexander of Macedonia wept because there were no more worlds to conquer. Pity he wasn't into business or industry, because they offer a much larger canvas—there will always be another world waiting, then another, and another.

After etching his name into the Powai workshop's history, Naik stepped outside. The stage shifted to a workshop that was geared for tomorrow—a workshop by the water.

The old management saying goes 'you need to be a leader of men before you become a leader of businesses'. Naik had already ticked one box. The subsequent chapters will tell us how he mastered the others.

**Postscript:** Many years after the events described in Powai, Gunnar Hansen, the glum and distinctly uncommunicative head of manufacturing in Powai, had risen high up the ladder to become deputy managing director. It so happened that he and Baker were reminiscing over a drink about the old days. Hansen turned to Baker and said: 'You know, Tim, if there's one good thing you have done for the company, it's having recruited Naik.'

'Bloody hell,' thought Baker to himself, 'he was arguing with me when I recruited Naik, and now he is thanking me.'

Time has told, and how!

# 2

# Hazira: From Marshland to Mega Engineering Complex

*'My focus is on building capability and not just capacity. Anybody with money can build capacity.'*

Sometimes it's banners that say it best. They capture the mood of the occasion and provide a succinct summation of a story. It was 1 December 2021, and many colourful banners fluttered in the gentle morning breeze blowing in from the river Tapti towards Hazira. The banners summed up the mood behind the function that was going to take place that day, carrying as they did a picture of Naik and reading: 'Honouring our history. Celebrating the moment.'

# A.M. Naik

Top executives of L&T and leaders drawn from its different businesses had flown in from Mumbai, as had the man of the moment, Naik.

The invitees, including these authors, gathered on the lawns outside Hazira's Strategic Business Unit (SBU) Block around a large plaque, which was hidden from public view behind rich, red velvet. At the appointed hour, the curtains parted, revealing a signboard that read 'A.M. Naik Heavy Engineering Complex'. The crowd cheered and broke into stentorian applause.

In a brief speech at the auditorium, L&T's chairman and managing director, S.N. Subrahmanyan, said it was a unanimous decision of the board of directors to honour Naik for his pivotal role in setting up the facility that had become a national asset. Later, several others, including Y.S. Trivedi—a seasoned veteran of L&T's giant Hazira facility—spoke about Naik's role in conceiving, incubating and setting it up. This function, he said, was simple—it was a campus honouring its creator.

Seated on stage, Naik would have replayed in his mind the long, accomplishment-studded history of the Hazira campus. It was a saga that went back to an eventful evening four decades ago, by the Tapti riverbank.

## From the muddy banks of the Tapti

Naik's gumboots squelched in the marsh and every ripple of the rising tide seemed to edge the riverbank farther and farther away. Plus, there were other things to worry about—in the swirling waters of a turbid river, you could never be sure of your foothold.

## Hazira: From Marshland to Mega Engineering Complex

It would have been easy to abort the mission and head back home, but Naik is not built that way. This was Hazira—the site he had scouted, identified, battled for and, finally, secured. And now that the time had come to examine the property, he would not leave until he had gone from end to end and studied the ebb and flow of the tides. You can ask yourself how many business leaders would cast aside their suit and tie and don gumboots to step into the ceaselessly shifting, silted riverbank. As in everything else, Naik wanted to know things first-hand and get a feel for them. He spent another hour wading through the waters before he was convinced. Yes, Hazira would work.

The story of the waterside facility in Hazira began not in its immediate vicinity but around 300 kilometres away in Powai, a suburb of Mumbai. Larsen & Toubro's sprawling workshops there, set up progressively in the 1940s and 1950s, were geared to build a wide range of plant and equipment for the power, petrochemical and chemical industries. The company's history books tell us that the first facility it set up was a small, rudimentary workshop on Calicut Street, a stone's throw from the original office at Mercantile Chambers in Ballard Estate. But if you were to discount that as insignificant, the sprawling complex near Powai was L&T's mother ship, and was virtually synonymous with the company.

Two decades since Naik's job interview in Powai, a lot had happened—industry had changed, technology had grown complex and Naik himself was no longer a junior engineer. He was now spearheading Group II, the large business group within L&T, and had high expectations from the manufacturing facility in terms of scale and complexity. Powai, it was clear, would not be able to cope.

It also had another limitation—it was landlocked. This meant that transporting large equipment (called over dimensional cargo, or ODC) was a logistical nightmare.

The search then began for a location with access to water, and soon was narrowed down to Surat on India's west coast—a historical gateway to sea trade. Silt from the Tapti may have pushed the city inland, but its far-flung suburb Hazira was on the river and would provide access to the Arabian Sea. A new future then began for Hazira, for the Tapti and, not least, for Naik.

From day one, Hazira was a vote of affirmation for the prowess and promise of India's indigenous manufacturing capability. It came at a time when received wisdom said all complex engineering equipment had to be made either in the West or in the Far East, and India had to satisfy itself with the simpler stuff—the slack. This went against the grain of those who conceived and nurtured Hazira, and so they began the long and difficult but professionally rewarding process of change. The workshops saw a level of commitment—and a matching level of investment—that would bring the facility on par with the finest in the industry globally. One line rang through the shops: 'If anyone in the world can do it, we can do it too. And at the next opportunity, we will do it better.'

Hazira's Manufacturing Successes: Manufacturing operations started in 1987 and the roles of those who were involved changed from project engineers to manufacturing supervisors. If there is a point at which you could place your finger and begin tracing Hazira's manufacturing journey, it would be with the manufacture in 1988–90 of the country's first hydrocracker reactor. Yes, hydrocrackers existed in India before, but this was the first one to carry the 'Made in India' label. It was a milestone and blazed a new trail, for it would be the precursor to the ultra-complex hydrocracker reactors of the future.

## New horizons at Hazira

From 1988 onwards, after securing the license to manufacture offshore platforms, Hazira started with a helideck before moving swiftly to offshore wellhead and process platforms. A year later came another benchmark—the manufacture of the prestigious 500 MWe Nuclear Reactors. Between 1991 and 1995, L&T's manufacturing team faced new and professionally exhilarating challenges. The team was raring to go. They looked forward to the opportunity to get their hands on new and complex steels. Why would anyone knowingly take on jobs that were tougher than anything ever done before? Perhaps the answer lies in Robert Frost's lines: 'I took [the road] less traveled by, and that has made all the difference.' For L&T's engineers and welding team, it did make a huge difference. From conventional manufacturing they were moving to the next level of high-tech manufacturing. The route that was followed was tried and tested: confront challenge; devise new solutions; develop inhouse technology, and, when everything else is in place, initiate the process of automation.

Those engaged in manufacturing of defence equipment were also conscious that they were at work for the Indian Navy and, at a larger level, for the nation. So if it meant arduous hours on the shop floor honing, testing and mastering new technologies, they were ready, willing, able. In the process, they also won for themselves a coveted badge—as a key private sector player in defence equipment manufacture.

As the years rolled on, manufacturing saw a continuous upgrade. A corporate decision was taken that Hazira would not manufacture any reactor below a high USD/kg threshold. It meant that manufacturing teams had to gear themselves up for high-tech reactors. There would be no soft options, no simple solutions. Necessity being the mother of many virtues, the teams rose to meet the challenge with elan. Then came a new challenge, or, as L&T's engineers chose to see it, a new canvas of opportunity. It came via the courts of law. The Supreme Court decreed that the citizens of the country were entitled to a breath of fresh air. Oil refineries were ordered to upgrade their standards. This led to a major, multi-locational order for L&T, which Naik's team took up. Here in Hazira, clean fuel technology led to the building of new types of reactors and systems for the country's refineries.

The search for greener, cleaner technologies is continuous. As we write this, L&T's new business—Green Manufacturing and Development—is participating in the global shift towards an environment-friendly future.

To get back to Hazira, from 2000 onwards, the learning curve went up and up. And the results they achieved were at par with, or often above, the benchmarks set by the original technology suppliers. One of the highlights was active participation in the manufacture of India's first nuclear-powered submarine, christened INS *Arihant*. It was tough going but they had Naik's support and encouragement throughout.

## Hazira: From Marshland to Mega Engineering Complex

When in the cyclic nature of things domestic orders began to ease up, the Hazira team sought new frontiers in terms of both geography and capability. The company forayed into markets beyond Indian shores. So began the long and richly rewarding story of hydrocracker reactors for international markets. Today 65 per cent of reactors made in Hazira are exported. That should not come as too much of a surprise since Hazira veterans claim that this facility on the banks of the Tapti is the best-equipped heavy engineering workshop in the world.

We thumbed through the pages of Hazira's history to find the FCC regenerator. This mountain of gleaming metal is a photogenic piece of equipment that has been splashed across the media along with the doughty ethylene oxide (EO) reactor. Both pieces of equipment are large and complex, built to stringent tolerances and demanding deadlines—the kind of challenge Hazira revels in. In 2007, the workshop successfully delivered the world's biggest EO reactor to Kuwait on a nomination basis. Today, the workshop commands a dominant share of the global market for EO reactors. In the heavy engineering space, as everyone knows, it is critical to secure approval from international technology suppliers; without it, you are out on a limb. Hazira won approval by demonstrating that it could make good on its claims. European companies reluctant to 'qualify' L&T in 2007 are now willing to partner it in manufacturing ultra-super heavy reactors.

The icing on the cake was the world's largest ever order for reactors—an order from Kuwait National Petroleum Corporation for twenty-two reactors.

# A.M. Naik

## Replicating the sun

In 2015 came another global benchmark—replicating the sun. It is a fascinating project involving mind-boggling numbers—the largest high-vacuum pressure vessel ever made in human history. It was being built for the International Thermonuclear Experimental Reactor (ITER).

The details of the cryostat order are worth going into, as they reveal an important side to Naik's character. Initially, he had reservations about the project—while he acknowledged it would be a technological feat for L&T to build the system, he was unsure of its prospects in pure business terms. Projects of this nature are discussed and debated intensely at then board level, and so was the ITER project. Its chief proponent was then board member M.V. Kotwal, known to be an ace technocrat. But when you are leading a business, you also need to keep the business risks in perspective, and this is what bothered Naik.

It was supposed to be a global research project, meaning there was no clear authority who would take responsibility in case things went wrong. There were multiple companies from seven countries, so again, there wasn't a single source of funding. To make the prospects even more wobbly, the massive structure was to be shipped to the south of France in fifty-two large parts and assembled close to the country's border with Switzerland. France was well-known, dare we say notorious, for the propensity of its worker unions to halt work on the slightest pretext. To Naik, in purely commercial terms, the project was riddled with uncertainties. But seeing the passion

## Hazira: From Marshland to Mega Engineering Complex

with which his two generals, M.V. Kotwal and A.V. Parab, were pursuing it, he nodded in assent.

How the cryostat came to be—from daring and difficult concept to successful completion—is a story that merits being featured in manuals of high-technology manufacturing. But we'll focus here on the happy twist at the end of this tough road.

The ITER had arranged for a celebratory function to mark the completion of manufacturing and to flag off the shipment. The heads of the various companies involved gave brief speeches. Naik was initially expected to only mouth the usual pleasantries, but he made a statement that still rings in the ears of all those in the audience.

Naik began by admitting he had initially been in two minds about taking part in the project and its commercial viability. Then, he said it was only Kotwal's passion and perseverance that saw it through. 'All credit to my colleague M.V. Kotwal and his team,' he said.

Kotwal himself had not expected this. 'I was touched,' he told us years later. 'Even now, I feel it was a great thing for Mr Naik to have said what he did.'

Naik never shies from admitting that he had nursed doubts about a project. Later, when proved wrong, nobody is happier than him. He then goes out of his way to give credit where it is due—hallmarks of a true leader.

### Armoured systems complex

Y.S. Trivedi was among the leaders hand-picked by Naik to turn his vision for Hazira into the magnificent reality now sprawling along the Tapti. In fact, Trivedi was the one entrusted by Naik to take possession of the land in October 1983—a distinction he says he's unlikely to ever forget.

A technologist who worked assiduously on almost everything that Naik assigned to him, he has grown into an exceptional, many-faceted professional. So multi-faceted is Trivedi that we must add as an aside that his personal library in Vadodara boasts luminaries from Adi Shankara to Franz Kafka. Of how many other hardcore engineers can you say that!

To return to Hazira, this facility has grown to become L&T's 'show window'—if you want to impress someone with the manufacturing capabilities of the company, take them to Hazira. Want to talk about scale? Hazira will show it better than any words can—its visitors' book reads like a who's who of political leadership, industry and society; it has rolled out the red carpet for the Prime Minister, the home minister, three defence ministers, the National Security Advisor, most past and present chairpersons of the organizations which lead India's three strategic sectors—the DAE (Department of Atomic Energy, Department of Space and Defence Research and Development Organisation) and a succession of high-profile leaders.

We see the giant Hazira complex as a reflection of Naik's personality—its large scale, its gutsy quest to build bigger, better and faster, and, most of all, its aspiration to meet the needs of the nation.

A new page to its story was added with the Armoured Systems Complex (called ASC by L&T employees, who have a penchant for abbreviating and initializing). This was dedicated to the nation

## Hazira: From Marshland to Mega Engineering Complex

by PM Narendra Modi on 19 January 2019, accompanied by Defence Minister Nirmala Sitharaman and the top leadership of the Ministry of Defence. The PM even took a ride in the howitzer. Promotional material released by the company on the occasion termed it 'Aatmanirbharta [self-reliance] in action', and, with an alliterative flourish, said it would provide 'might, mind and muscle' for India's defence.

### A battlefield minus the shooting

The ASC looks like a slice of a battlefield, minus the live shooting. Its testing tracks have steep gradients, ditches, water trenches—almost everything a howitzer is likely to encounter when it confronts the enemy.

For the uninitiated, it must be clarified that although a howitzer looks like a conventional battle tank, it is an entirely different animal—tanks belong to the infantry; howitzers are part of the artillery.

The Hazira ASC is where the first batch of 100 K9 Vajra-T howitzers were manufactured. To understand more about the gun, we went to meet the man who was then in charge of the business—J.D. Patil, a gold medallist M.Tech. from IIT, whose speciality is the technology that animates weaponry.

Patil began by telling us that L&T doesn't handle ammunition. It also doesn't make anti-personnel mines, he said. For the company, it is just the technology that is involved. The K9 Vajra-T, he said, was a valuable asset for the army on all fronts. L&T engineers had carried out design modifications on the original Korean gun, making it better suited for desert warfare, able to fire a variety of ammunition. The team also worked on making the guns suitable for mountain warfare. Anyone aware of India's geopolitical realities will know why and where the country needs those guns. The howitzers were delivered ahead of schedule. It was a cheery moment for all when the Chief of Army Staff announced that the guns had exceeded expectations. More guns are on their way.

Patil said the ASC embodies a spirit dear to Naik's heart, 'Make in India', and added that when the high-calibre howitzers go out to battle the enemy and defend the nation's interests, it will be a matter of pride for every L&T employee that it all began in the A.M. Naik Heavy Engineering Complex.

In the course of our extended visit to Hazira, we had the good fortune of running into Atik Desai, a former senior executive who had literally evolved with the campus. Atikbhai—as he is known around the plant—was in a position to give us a historical perspective. He had joined L&T as a junior manager—a rank considerably below his position he held with his previous employer, the Tatas. He had also sacrificed on emoluments. It struck us that his rationale was somewhat similar to A.M. Naik's when he had said 'yes' to Baker's downsized offer. 'For me, it was not about position or salary, it was about people and purpose.'

Atik Desai speaks earnestly and at length about the formative years. He told us that all the engineers who laid the foundations of the facility at Hazira had been handpicked by Naik. 'A facility is ultimately as successful as its leaders. If you don't have a proper leader, you won't grow. Naik saab is the leader who had mapped out Hazira thoroughly in his mind before implementation began.

## Hazira: From Marshland to Mega Engineering Complex

Almost everything went as per his plan—from the location of the machinery to the framing of the standing orders of facility.'

Like every other business, heavy engineering too has its ups and downs, and the trick to success and sustainable growth is to make sure that the ups outnumber and outweigh the downs. One man who has seen both the highs and the lows is the genial, high-octane Falgun Chokshi. He told us about Naik's uncanny ability to anticipate the likely shape of things to come. 'In 1983, no one could imagine the kind of jobs we are doing now. Typically, the maximum diameter of a job could be 4–5 metres. Here we do 16 metres, 20 metres. It was classic Imagineering by Naik saab.'

Permit us a brief digression to get to the roots of the portmanteau word 'imagineering' that Chokshi used. It means the bold act of imagining the seemingly impossible and then engineering it into reality. The word once formed part of the tagline used by L&T in its advertising campaign in the early part of this century: 'It's all about imagineering'. When the advertisements were released, some people were apprehensive that the word carried a Walt Disney copyright. In reality, whatever its origins, the word had since been featured in dictionaries and passed into public usage. L&T had taken the precaution of copyrighting its tagline.

To return to our interview, Chokshi told us about how Naik relentlessly raises the bar. 'When I joined in 1991, there was only one heavy engineering shop at Hazira. Today there are six. At a time when we were thinking how to run three shops to full capacity, and when you are struggling to make that happen, Mr Naik would step in only to add two more shops. That's the kind of leader he is—he challenges you to keep pace.'

Naik was the one behind the setting up of a super heavy shop with a lifting capacity of up to 1,000 tonnes. 'This kind of lifting capacity does not exist in this part of the world. When I bring clients here, they are dumbfounded. That's vision, that's Naik. And to think all this was marsh!'

Similar sentiments were expressed by battle-hardened L&T veterans, Sanjay Desai and Satish Palekar. Palekar told us that in his mentoring sessions, Naik can teach a person all that they will not learn at Harvard. He narrated how Naik once told him: 'There is a scientific and mathematical way to take decisions. Unless your instinct and gut are aligned, you cannot take a right decision. Up to around 75 per cent to 80 per cent, you can rely on your math, and the remaining is gut, based on experience and knowledge. If you don't use your gut feel, you won't take a decision, and you will regret it. If you do, go ahead and take the risk, and it will be worth it.'

**The smart factory**

Digitalization is the new buzzword changing the way manufacturing is done around the world. Hazira is quick off the mark when it comes to identifying and adopting new technology trends like the internet of things (more sharply defined as the industrial internet of things, IIoT). While its engineers and technicians may be happy with their long history of accomplishment, there are new peaks that remain to be scaled. It is a long mountain range. And while Naik may not be directly involved in pushing the IoT across the workshops that bear his name, he stands back and watches

## Hazira: From Marshland to Mega Engineering Complex

with pride as the seeds he sowed decades ago bring in a rich and diverse harvest.

Hazira is now full of innovative new systems that would require an entire book to explain. So, instead, we focused on a system with an interesting name, FIGGY, which is an integrated online mechanism developed to take care of supplies—flux and wires—used in welding. It has made the process error-proof.

Beginning in 2019, Hazira has IoT-ized all its head welding stations. An IoT-ized welding station resembles a booth with see-through walls, where all controls are on a single console. The outcome is that while earlier a welder and an assistant could undertake arcing for four hours, now the welder alone can do it for six and a half to eight hours, and the assistant is dispensed with.

To those who do not know him, Naik would seem to be the sort of person who would believe in 'old is gold' and frown at new and unfamiliar ways of doing things. But, in fact, he is the exact opposite—he is more welcoming of new trends than youngsters half his age. He knows that you cannot press 'pause' on evolution. It is important to keep pace with change.

This belief of Naik's has changed large sections of Hazira, including defence, hydrocarbon engineering, boilers, turbine generators and the forgings shop. That is why walking into any shop floor in Hazira is like walking into the future—there seems to be at least one robotic welder on every floor. Robots can handle weights up to 2.5 metric tonnes and work six times faster than a human being.

These new facets of Hazira's growth have also attracted the attention of the media. In a report headlined 'Factory Floors

# A.M. Naik

Turning New Frontiers for Digitisation', a leading publication said: 'The push towards Industry 4.0 is prompting Indian conglomerates and large companies—such as Larsen & Toubro ... to ramp up investments to optimize operations and boost productivity... All the factory automation that we saw around us was being driven by data. It has led to a reduction in the cycle time for welding and also driven down manpower costs. The money saved is ploughed back to making factories smarter.'

We wondered about the impact of all this automation, digitalization and artificial intelligence on the role of human beings in manufacturing. Do they have a future at all? It is a question that is being asked by many. The answer, or at least a part of it, came to us as we stood on the bank of the Tapti as it curled past a river island. The sunlight was fading, and on the far side, halogen lamps had begun to come into play. These pinpricks of light would hold the darkness at bay until the sun rose again.

The answer is that we need to be patient and perseverant. Of course, human beings will always be needed, for they are the ones who can dream. Then, they'll begin acting on that dream. They will plan to build, among other things, better and smarter robots. They will encounter challenges and will grow by overcoming them.

Just like one inspirational figure did many decades ago, trudging along the marshy banks of the river Tapti in gumboots, dedicated young men and women will build a new tomorrow.

# 3

# One Battle, Many Victories

*'From every crisis that we encountered, we have emerged stronger.'*

As the long-drawn, hard-fought corporate battle drew to a close, it was time for the generals to shake hands. Kumar Mangalam Birla, chairman and scion of one of the country's largest global conglomerates, the Aditya Birla Group, held his hand out to A.M. Naik, who had led L&T to an unexpected victory.

'Mr Naik, do you realize what you have done? You have made sure that L&T is not easily taken over,' Birla said. Naik smiled modestly.

'When the history of L&T is written, your name should be inscribed in letters of gold,' continued Birla. How prophetic those words would be!

## A.M. Naik

The battle that had just concluded had originated before either of the 'generals' themselves had entered the scene. By the mid-1980s, L&T had become one of the more respected engineering companies in corporate India. It was large, had developed remarkable engineering and construction capability, and employed a sizeable, talented workforce, led by thoroughbred professionals. But it was vulnerable—a loosely held company with widely dispersed shareholding.

This was an Achilles heel that had remained hidden from public gaze until it was brought to light in the aggressive, acquisitive business climate of the late 1980s. The company became tempting prey for buccaneer business leaders in search of a quick buck, corporate raiders whose modus operandi was to rapidly acquire a controlling stake in target companies and then proceed to put their hands in the till.

One such corporate raider, with a fearsome track record of seizing control of profit-making companies, was Manu Chhabria, who had made his vast fortune in the Gulf states as an agent for foreign manufacturers of consumer electronics.

When he first turned his eye towards L&T, alarm bells went off in the boardroom. In corporate circles, hearing the name of Manu Chhabria was akin to an ancient king getting word that the Huns were headed in his kingdom's direction.

Only a year ago in 1988, N.M. Desai, L&T's chairman and managing director at the time, had celebrated its golden jubilee at a glitzy function in Mumbai (then called Bombay). Few among the rollicking executives who had gathered for the event would have known that a minefield lay in their path. Desai soon recognized the threat for what it was and tried gamely to fend it off. In his hour of crisis, a white knight appeared in the form of a trailblazing businessman who was rapidly making a name for himself in industrial circles—Dhirubhai Ambani. Dhirubhai was in the process of decisively rewriting the rules of the game in Indian industry. He acquired a sizeable stake in L&T, triggering a period of flux and uncertainty. But none of it had much of an impact on the performance of the company. L&T continued on its planned, if somewhat placid, trajectory of growth. The Ambanis faced resistance from a section of the stakeholders, and while they managed to retain their holding in L&T, they had to cede control. The never-say-die company, however, soon found a buyer in another family business group—the Birlas. This large and storied business family had major plans for growth and expansion in cement, and L&T was a coveted acquisition. They took Ambani's holding and looked for more to clinch their acquisition.

**Lone crusader**

Nothing seemed to be able to stop them except for one stubborn leader with the gumption and the guts to stand in their way. Now, chieftains of family-run conglomerates tend to look with a curious mixture of emotions upon executives who have risen up the ranks. The executives are no doubt respected for expertise in their chosen domains, but it is felt that fighting an inter-corporate battle is quite beyond them.

They are usually at a loss, not knowing what to do, whom to approach in the corridors of power or how to safeguard their controlling interests. But Naik turned out to be very different from the typical white-collar executive.

Right from the start, he was upfront and made his intentions clear—he was opposed to any attempt at a takeover. But you don't step on to the battlefield without raising an army. Given the delicate nature of the issue, there wasn't much of an army—Naik had only two lieutenants, and even they were only informed of developments on a need-to-know basis.

However, former US Secretary of Defense Donald Rumsfeld once said, 'You go to war with the army you have.' And so, Naik and his lieutenants prepared themselves for what was going to be a long and complex phase.

A lot had to be done, much of it in the corridors of the North Block in the country's capital, where the destinies of corporates can be made or unmade.

Naik flew to Delhi to muster support; at that time, North Block was unfamiliar territory to him. In the high-stakes game of influence peddling, L&T had been a novice, unlike family-owned organizations, for whose satraps it was customary to cultivate the powers that be. But Naik was transparent and passionate about his cause. There was always some support to be found for a lone individual battling an organization, and Naik deftly tapped into it.

Outside L&T, those in support of the battle against the takeover included the redoubtable crusader for corporate ethics and nationalism S. Gurumurthy. A canny, razor-sharp corporate adviser, Gurumurthy emerged as a dragon slayer in the 1980s. He was known to take a principled stand against all odds and against the all-powerful. Gurumurthy, in tandem with Arun Shourie, former

## One Battle, Many Victories

editor of *The Indian Express*, wrote multiple detailed articles about the attempt in the late 1980s to seize control of L&T. Now, some two decades later, Gurumurthy had lost none of his appetite for a good fight when yet another attempt was made to take over L&T. But his role was different this time and there was another aspect to Gurumurthy's involvement. He was on good terms with the Birlas, and so had the ear of both parties—the family conglomerate as well as Naik. More importantly he was also close to Prime Minister Atal Bihari Vajpayee and Finance Minister Jaswant Singh, with whom he had long and friendly relations.

At that point, the Birlas had increased their stake in L&T to 16 per cent. And thus began the corporate-cum-political war. The acquisition battle became more intricate and more heated. Many observers felt that it was only a matter of time before L&T capitulated. After all, in a high-stakes battle, what could a group of professionals—a David—do against the Goliaths seasoned in dealing with fellow industrialists, bureaucrats and key decision-makers in the government? That the unequal struggle would soon end and L&T would be absorbed into the Birla fold, another vessel in the vast Birla armada, was the assessment of the corporate world and in the government ecosystem. If that happened, the culture, the unique ethos that set this company apart from the rest would vanish.

Naik was a newcomer to this game; he knew virtually next to nobody in the corridors of power. In these places, what matters more than who you are is whom you know. But when Naik met ministers, he did not have the contacts he could leverage, nor friends he could mobilize in support. On all the things that mattered in a power game, Naik was at a disadvantage. But he had one secret weapon hidden in himself. One weapon more powerful than all the contacts one could muster. That was his passion for L&T. His unswerving loyalty to L&T was obvious to all. But, would passion alone work? Many said it wouldn't, but it did.

He approached those who were touched by his deep feelings. Gurumurthy, who had helped L&T earlier, was one of them. Naik sought Gurumurthy's advice. The first thing Gurumurthy did was petition the government to halt the ominous acquisitions. He said that anyone in the system would know that one wouldn't buy 16 per cent of a company to just watch the values grow. That was how the system got alerted to the happenings in L&T.

Gurumurthy told us that although Naik was an executive of L&T, he possessed a sense of its ownership was superior to the sense of ownership that a proprietor has. The company had no proprietor and no promoter; its employees were, so to speak, its emotional owners. In Naik, they found their most passionate and eloquent champion.

As we have said earlier, Gurumurthy was close to all parties concerned—the Birlas, L&T and the government. His words and views carried a lot of weight with all. 'I spoke to [then Prime Minister] Vajpayee and told him that L&T was a national asset and needed to be protected. Vajpayee agreed and asked me to meet Jaswant Singh, the finance minister. When they asked what I felt needed to be done to save L&T, I told the government that Naik had forethought everything: what should be done and who had to do what. All that he wanted was "the blessings of the government". The government, which was one of the most honest ones since Independence, gladly did in public interest and for no other consideration all that Naik wanted. When the Birla–L&T demerger deal was announced, the entire media reported it as win-win for both.'

Gurumurthy said that although he does not admire a person very easily, he soon became and remains 'a great admirer of Naik.' He went on to describe how the two bonded: 'Our relationship grew because like me Naik is a staunch nationalist. He has never seen L&T as a corporate but as part of the larger idea of India.' He added, 'I never had any kind of professional relationship with L&T at any point and was just Naik's friend and admirer. Later, when Naik wanted me to be on the L&T board as an independent director, I told him I do not accept any position in any corporate.'

## The win-win ending

One of Naik's two trusted lieutenants mentioned before was N. Sivaraman, who has since left L&T but continues to stay in touch with his former boss. Recalling his own role in the financial negotiations, he told us: 'I took tough calls on certain matters of finance. Mr Birla complained about me to Mr Naik, saying I was not willing to be flexible. Then, in Mr Birla's presence, I explained my position. Mr Naik said he would go by my decision. That is the kind of leader that he is—he may take you to task privately, but in the presence of others, he stands by his people.'

The takeover episode ended happily. Right from the start, the Birlas had set their sights on L&T's cement business, and they got what they were looking for. As for L&T, it also got what it wanted most—freedom.

M. Damodaran, former chairman of the Unit Trust of India, and a former member of L&T's board of directors, is acknowledged across industry as a brand ambassador of good governance. Fresh-faced and thorough going, he is the kind of person who is comfortably at ease in every corporate situation. With his seemingly instinctive ability to analyse issues, Damodaran threw light on something we had not thought of before. 'Naik had no skin in the game. He wasn't doing it because he had a personal agenda. A lot of professionals would not have got their hands dirty. They would simply say, 'what's in it for me?'. They would walk away from battle and let the corporates settle their issues between themselves,' he said.

'They would think "Whether it's the Ambanis or the Birlas, at the end of the day, they will come back to me and ask me to run the company. They have done it before, and they will do it again. I am an employee, so it makes no difference to me who the owners are,"' he added.

But Naik did not look at it through that prism at all. He was not fighting for himself; he was fighting for history. If either of the two family conglomerates gained control, his personal future would be unaffected, but L&T, as we know it, would cease to exist. Its unique character, its freedom and its distinction from all the rest would be erased. It would not then be the independent nation-builder that had drawn the young career aspirant to L&T's gates four decades ago. It is important to highlight here that L&T continues to enjoy the respect of the companies it had earlier confronted. All the contending parties continue as its valued customers. Few business books can offer a better illustration of the concept of 'win-win'.

The Birla battle would become one of many Naik fought across his decades at the helm, and each of them is illustrative of his courage, the thoroughness of his strategies and, in the face of a crisis, his refusal to give in.

## A track record of courage

Naik has always been gutsy, and those who have read his biography *The Nationalist* will know how many times he has demonstrated it in the past.

Some incidents from his younger days serve as prime examples, such as when Naik rallied students against a school authority, leading to the reinstatement of an English teacher whom the students looked up to.

In college, his courage came to the fore when he stood up to intimidation during a contentious student election. One afternoon, the local bully walked up to him and asked: 'Are you planning to stand for the general secretary's post?'

'Maybe,' Naik replied cryptically.

'See, I am going to stand,' replied the young tough. 'It will be better for you if you withdraw gracefully. Know what I mean?'

Naik looked the bully straight in the eye. 'I was in two minds on whether to contest or not. But now that you are threatening me, I have made up my mind. I will contest,' he said.

Naik was general secretary for the better part of his college years, and gained priceless experience leading the students' union.

Then, at the start of his professional career, it was courage that made Naik the only officer with the gumption to walk on to the shop floor after dark.

He had been counselled against it as it was 'not safe'. A cautious 'safety first' approach would have made him stay away from danger. But Naik being Naik, he decided to do exactly the opposite, and walked into the plant—first at 8 p.m. and then at 10 p.m. Nothing happened. Then, he ventured into the den at midnight and started pulling up slackers in the cloakroom—something he is still remembered for.

We do not know if he had ever heard of the famous lines by Plato: 'Courage is a kind of salvation. Courage is knowing what not to fear.' But he did put similar thoughts to practice.

In business too Naik followed the same process of taking actions that dwarfed precedent. They were just never done before. He got out of areas that were not 'core' to L&T. While many know of the multiple businesses into which Naik boldly led the company, the list of non-core activities that the company divested is equally impressive.

There was a time when L&T was closely identified with cement. Remember the lines 'The trust you have in L&T, now in L&T cement'? But as we have just recorded, Naik got out of the business, weathering murmurs of opposition. Other examples include exiting the businesses of developing maintenance welding electrodes, plastics processing, foundry and, of course, electrical and automation systems in 2020. None of these were easy decisions to take because, on the face of it, all were making profits. But Naik looked beyond the immediate and concluded that they did not fit into L&T's long-term goals. So, he forged ahead, waiting calmly for history to prove him right. After a while, doing things that were never done before became the norm for him.

At every level, Naik found within himself the strength needed to overcome the challenge.

## The biggest of many victories

The Birla episode was a battle with many victories. One of them, probably the most significant, was that when the dust settled, Naik held in hand a cherished prize—the opportunity to ring-fence L&T from takeovers and give the company's employees the liberty to determine their own destiny. This led to the setting up of the Employee Welfare Trust. It needed a karta, a doer. Naik sought a person of unique stature.

He went to meet the ninety-four-year-old co-founder of the company, Henning Holck-Larsen. Ageing and infirm, Holck-Larsen asked Naik if this trust, of which he would become a signatory, would help the employees. When Naik said it definitely would, Holck-Larsen smilingly gave his assent.

Naik then called on N.M. Desai, another pillar around whom the company was built. Desai gave his assent too. The benedictions of both these fabled leaders had positive results far into the future, and today, the trust offers financial assistance to former and current employees to help them meet medical expenses. This is over and above what they receive through the company's medical schemes.

The trust also provides scholarships to students for graduate and postgraduate studies. And when employees' children want to make a name for themselves on the sports field, the trust is at hand with scholarships and help in training.

All this is in addition to the core objective that lies at the heart of the trust—to protect L&T from corporate predators. The trust now owns around 14 per cent of the equity in L&T, acting as its protective shield. Naik ranks this as one of his life's most prized accomplishments.

As we said at the start of this chapter, it was one battle that paved the way for many victories. As for the victorious general, he was soon back on the field, gazing into the horizon for fresh battles.

# 4
# The New L&T

*'We will pursue our business goals and constantly add value to all our stakeholders while serving the larger national cause.'*

'WHAT YOU HAVE ACHIEVED FOR L&T IS BEYOND WHAT I COULD have imagined.' That succinct tribute to A.M. Naik's contribution came from the late N.M. Desai—L&T's venerable former chairman and managing director, the first Indian to occupy that post. We had interviewed Desai when he was in his nineties. He was ailing and found it difficult to speak for any length of time. But he said it all in that one single sentence.

What exactly were the achievements that Desai was referring to? It was the new character of the company and its new acquisitions.

## A.M. Naik

With a sweeping gesture of his hand, Naik tells us, '92 per cent of the L&T you see around you was not there in its present shape and size before I stepped in. The other 8 per cent is what I inherited from my predecessors.'

This may sound boastful, but it is not pride; it is passion. Naik is so immersed, so inextricably engaged in what he is doing that he wants entrenched perceptions of L&T to be overhauled and the prevailing reality to be recognized.

Naik has relevant facts and figures at his fingertips—the claim of having built 92 per cent of the company is well-studied, verifiable and widely acknowledged. S.N. Subrahmanyan once remarked at an annual general meeting a couple of years ago that Naik 'has taken L&T up and brought it to where it is today'. Subramanian Sarma, a director on the L&T board, told us that while the claim of 92 per cent may sound incredible, Naik 'can back it up to the last decimal'.

That is why the company's shareholders unfailingly clamour for suitable recognition for Naik's massive contribution. At the AGM we attended, shareholders suggested a change of name—they wanted the ampersand in L&T replaced with an 'N', and the company to be officially renamed 'Larsen Naik Toubro'. We were told this is a familiar demand that crops up at every AGM. But Naik himself wants none of it; he smiles but never concedes to the request. His matter-of-fact answer is that 'L&T, as it stands, is a super brand, a global brand. Any change will cause confusion, so we will respect the status quo.'

The sentiments behind the shareholders' demand are expressed differently by many. Former director V.K. Magapu, who has a gift for the mot juste, said: 'If Henning Holck-Larsen and Søren Kristian Toubro are the co-founders of the company, Mr Naik is the re-founder of L&T.'

So, where did this 're-finding' begin? For the answer, we need to turn back the pages of history to 1999.

## Big bang

In late April of that year, there was a vigorous buzz across L&T's offices—A.M. Naik was going to be the next CEO and managing director. It wasn't much of a surprise because Naik had been a strong candidate for the top job five years earlier too. But this time, it was a virtual certainty.

Still, by the time the official circular announced the appointment, everyone had braced themselves for a brand-new era. They knew that change, both immediate and long-term, was on its way.

Naik's reputation preceded him to the post. As vice president on the board in-charge of the high-performance business cluster, covering heavy engineering and hydrocarbon projects and equipment, he had carved a niche for himself with the breathtaking scale of his projects, the speed of execution and enviable profitability. Everyone in L&T guessed correctly that it was not going to be 'business as usual' anymore.

Leaders face two options when they take over the reins of an organization. The first option, the easy one, is for CEOs to begin slowly, going with the flow in the early days and dispensing changes in small, regulated doses. But Naik chose the harder path—he had neither the patience nor the temperament for the other kind of approach. He was prepared not only to rock the boat but also to set the whole fleet on an entirely different course. No 'gentle' change of direction for him; he was the 'big bang' boss.

The first indications of what lay in store came through a series of letters on his new CEO letterhead. So many things began happening swiftly, simultaneously and in concert that many people began to wonder if Naik had readied himself for this eventuality. In truth, he had. He set out what he intended to do, even while his official appointment lay in the realm of uncertainty.

The new L&T is different not only in its composition but also in its character. The old hesitancy is gone, replaced by a confidence born of hard-won experience. It is almost like saying 'there is nothing too big for us to handle'.

**Engagement—Bachchan style**

To understand the scale of Naik's contribution to L&T, we turned to a man who once held the apex administrative position in India, cabinet secretary. Many key government decisions pivoted on him. Later, he served on L&T's board for several years, and even after retiring, he continued to stay in close touch with Naik.

S. Rajgopal is a man of few words and he provided the kind of insight that is best described as 'magisterial' in the course of an interview at his apartment high above the tri-junction opposite the Mantralaya in Mumbai. Rajgopal unveiled a fascinating portrait of Naik—the visionary, the entrepreneur and the social do-gooder.

## The New L&T

'Naik is our home-grown corporate czar,' said Rajgopal. 'He studied in a rural school in his hometown, which his father had developed. Plus, he did not go abroad for studies; he went to a local school, and not even an English-medium one. Then, to an indigenous engineering college.'

The import of his words was obvious: success and high achievement are not the products of the institutions you attend; they are shaped by what lies within you.

'As a business leader, you need to be adept at playing the corporate game,' continued Rajgopal. 'Naik knows how to grow the company in tune with national aspirations, protect it against the competition and do it all on ethical lines.' This, Rajgopal believes, is one of Naik's most significant achievements, and there is a lot that business aspirants can learn from his methods.

There is also, of course, his total involvement with the interests of the company. In a witty aside, Rajgopal described it as: 'We've all seen Amitabh Bachchan in the Bollywood film *Namak Halaal* going: "I can talk English, I can walk English, I can laugh English." In the same vein, I will say about Mr Naik that he sleeps L&T, walks L&T, breathes L&T.'

Like a chess grandmaster plotting his moves in advance, Naik drew up what he refers to as his 100-day plan. Not only was it all-encompassing in scope, but it was also precise in details. Those familiar with Naik would immediately recognize this as a character trait of his—every plan he has ever drawn up is accompanied by detailed instructions on how to go about implementing it.

We are not getting into the nitty-gritty of the 100-day plan, because that would require a whole manual. However, a glance at the plan was enough to show us that it mapped all points of significance for an organization in the throes of radical change.

A major milestone in the new CEO's journey was the formulation of a vision for L&T. This was historic and unprecedented. There had been some abstruse corporate dos and don'ts, but they did not possess the cogency of a vision statement. This would be the first, and it firmly set the compass in the direction the company would take. It also changed its growth trajectory and velocity. If ever there was a blueprint with 'transformation' written all over it, this was it.

Naik wanted to make sure that all the employees knew of the new vision and understood its implications. It wasn't enough that they had a vision statement displayed in all the conference rooms and printed in the corporate literature. Every employee had to 'own' the company's vision. So, he got together a core group of senior employees, who dotted the i's and crossed the t's, and made the statement the bedrock of collective belief. It is a roadmap and a reference book—when in doubt, refer to the vision statement; if further confirmation is needed, consult the strategic plan.

Changes in behaviour are often preceded by changes in lexicon, and at L&T, among the new phrases that Naik brought in was 'value creation'. According to the company's chief financial officer and member of the board, R. Shankar Raman: 'Mr Naik was the first to introduce to L&T's lexicon the words "shareholder value".'

It was not as if L&T had previously been doing something that was value non-accretive; Shankar Raman explained, it was actually a lack of prime focus. 'We were all working very hard; we were all going after whatever we were tasked with. But we didn't really connect the dots. Naik helped us get our act together and gave purpose to the pursuit. We are here to add "shareholder value".'

The CFO said the full meaning of the new mantra did not quite sink in at first. 'Little did I realize then that it is such a powerful, profound statement. It actually acts as a defence, securing the company from predators,' he added.

This marked a radical departure from precedent and became the prism through which every aspect of L&T was viewed. 'Is it creating value?' became the new standard by which every process would be measured.

We soon got to know Naik's idea of the characteristics of a professional entrepreneur. A professional is one who adds value to the organization. While this is good, Naik believes it is not good enough. An entrepreneur, on the other hand, multiplies value. Ultimately, it all boils down to how much value you are bringing to the table.

The transformation that Naik brought about was the outcome of a carefully thought-out plan, which had been deliberated upon, reviewed intensively and, when the time came, implemented rigorously. It embodied Naik's objectives of where he wanted to lead the company—it was grounded in reality, taking into account the prevailing industrial economic situation; it was firm and unyielding where needed, yet flexible enough to allow for the vicissitudes of an unpredictable global future.

To understand the evolution of L&T's strategic plan in full, we turned to Pathik R. Kothari (or 'PRK'), the name most closely associated with the articulation of the watershed plan apart from Naik himself. Kothari has a calm, equable demeanour, and it seems that no corporate disruption can upset his zen-like poise. But we can bet that like the proverbial swan, he paddles furiously out of sight.

For decades, Kothari has translated Naik's thoughts into an implementable plan. Indeed, one company insider joked 'PRK is our Vyasa', a reference to the mythological sage who is credited as the chronicler of the Mahabharata and the man who split the single, eternal Veda into four separate books—Rigveda, Yajurveda, Samaveda and Atharvaveda. Kothari is adept at instituting processes, building consensus and orchestrating a dozen different agencies to come together and give visible shape to the strategic plan.

According to many in the company, among the things he helped to do when the plan was in its infancy was christen it. Initially, it was referred to by the name of the management consultancy assisting in formulating it, say, for instance, 'XYZ Strategic Plan'. But that would be plain vanilla, lacking distinction and striking no chord. In marketing terms, strategic plans are a commodity, and L&T wanted something that was its own; it wanted a brand name.

Kothari persuaded the core group of senior L&T executives that a name would create affection and attachment. He asked the group: 'What do you want the new L&T to be? What are the characteristics you are looking for?' Suggestions began to pour in—some said 'growth' and 'profits', and others chipped in with 'innovation' and 'caring'. Weaving all these strands together, the name chosen was 'LAKSHYA'.

Precisely whose coinage was it? While others give him credit for it, Kothari himself shook his head when we asked him about it. 'No, I did not create it. I recall there was a line in some TV programme those days that became popular with the team. So when someone in the group suggested it, everyone else agreed,' he said.

The name still stands, although it is no longer seen as an acronym and has become accepted as a word signifying the goals that the company sets for itself. All subsequent editions of the plan changed the number suffixed to it—LAKSHYA-1, LAKSHYA-2, etc. When we said it was a pity that the person who gave the name is lost to anonymity, Kothari shrugged his shoulders—an L&T employee's typical gesture of dismissal—and said: 'We shouldn't be bothering too much about the author or the creator. "Who" is a matter of detail. What's important is that the word encompasses all the aspects we need to cover.'

## What is LAKSHYA?

The 'L' stands for 'lean'. At the time, L&T was widely thought to be heavy-footed, even ponderous. That had to change. The company under Naik would shed flab and start transforming into the proverbial lean, mean fighting machine.

The 'A' is for 'agile'. You can be lean, you can even drive yourself to emaciation, but you can still be slow. That wouldn't help; agility is vital. In a world that is changing continuously, it is important for organizations to be quick on their feet. They need to be able to seize an opportunity when it presents itself, respond with alacrity when they perceive threats and remain sensitive to all that is happening in the external world.

The 'K' stands for something fairly obvious because it is L&T's trump card—'knowledge'. In the ranking system of industry, knowledge is on the top rung, and L&T's expertise is especially prized because it comes packaged with the ability to make, build and execute. The LAKSHYA planners had identified knowledge as one of L&T's strengths, and aimed to build further on it, following the old maxim of doing more of what you do well. So strong is this emphasis on augmenting the existing knowledge base that company insiders joke that the 'L' and the 'T' in their organization's name stand for 'learning' and 'training'!

'S' is for 'speed' and 'scale'. Whatever you are doing—planning or manufacturing or developing expertise—what is non-negotiable is that you should do it quickly. As Dave Girouard, founder of high-profile AI-based lending platform Upstart, said: 'Speed is the ultimate weapon in business. All else being equal, the fastest company in any market will win.' In the pre-Naik era, L&T was known for many good things, but not speed. The new CEO brought in radical change, putting his foot on the accelerator and never taking it off. For Naik, speed goes hand in hand with another 'S' word—'scale'. Incremental changes would no longer be enough; he was looking for quantum jumps.

The 'H' stands for 'humane'. At first glance, this may seem at variance with all the other qualities listed so far. But upon further reflection, we realized that it was a typical L&T characteristic. This organization has won admiration for its accomplishments and respect for the values that stand at its core. In a world that is getting increasingly corporatized, where maximizing profits seems to be the only goal, L&T is known to possess heart and soul. Some companies could have jettisoned social responsibilities in the pursuit of business-oriented goals, but L&T did not succumb to the temptation. Humane it was, and humane it will stay.

The next letter is not as easily understood as the previous five—the 'Y' stands for 'yielding', but not in the sense of giving up; rather, it means what is produced, like in the term 'yield on investment'. In L&T's case, it is clear that the strategic plan is focused on yielding greater value. As Naik urged employees in all his speeches at that time: 'We need to constantly create value in everything we do.'

The final 'A' is a call to 'action'. Without this, all the preceding qualities would only be an academic dissertation on, say, the seven habits of successful conglomerates. But Naik is not one for such discussions; he was looking for visible, tangible action.

As acronyms go, LAKSHYA may not be a lexicographer's delight; some of the words seem force-fitted, and the concepts themselves could appear repetitive. We are informed that in the early days, there were those who pooh-poohed the new creation, predicting that it would never find resonance with the mass of employees. But those who came to mock remained to applaud, and LAKSHYA has now been firmly embedded into L&T's lexicon and its history.

For the man who built tomorrow, LAKSHYA was a tool and a touchstone.

## Implementing the plan

J.P. Nayak, former director on the L&T board, threw some light on the process by which the new CEO began rolling out transformation. Naik, he said, assigned roles and responsibilities to each of his colleagues on the board.

## A.M. Naik

'I was assigned the task of looking at strategic planning. The brief was: "Let's find out the metric by which we, as the directors, will be measured by the outside world." We make plans, we make sure that revenue goes up, we make sure that the cost comes down, we make sure that the profit goes up… But how does the outside world measure us?'

The answer is market capitalization. Nayak recalls the CEO telling him: 'Let's find out ways and means whereby we can multiply it ten times, twenty times, a hundred times.' In recent times, those who follow the stock market will know that the L&T stock has seen encouraging growth. Part of the reason is that the seeds were sown very well by Naik.

It was a mantra that had spectacular outcomes. Between 1999 and 2023, group revenues grew from ₹5,000 crore to nearly ₹1,83,000 crore on a like-to-like basis. This surge, achieved largely through organic growth, has few parallels in corporate India. In the same period, market cap climbed from around ₹4,000 crore to around ₹3,74,000 crore at a compound annual growth rate (CAGR) of nearly 20 per cent.

This has enabled L&T to issue bonuses to shareholders four times, in addition to the handsome dividends they receive every year. So one share twenty years ago is equivalent to nine shares as of today.

You can't create value unless you have the right kind of people. High on the agenda of the 100-day plan, therefore, was making L&T a purely merit-based company. As Naik animatedly puts it, 'merit, merit and merit alone should prevail'. This was intended to counter the impression gaining ground that L&T had become a hierarchical organization, where how senior you were mattered more than how well you did your job.

Sounds familiar? It is the bane of many large organizations. At L&T, it would probably have been recognized even earlier as a disincentive to performance by previous leaders. But what held them back from taking remedial measures was the uncertainty of possible consequences. Naik knew no such fears—if something had to be done for the long-term good of the organization, Naik was ready to bite the bullet. He had always regarded human resources (HR) as the driving force of an organization, and he was about to shift to top gear.

P. R. Kothari said that earlier, HR was treated as just another service department of the organization. Under Naik, it was put under the spotlight. He revamped its processes, with an overriding emphasis on merit, and gave the performance appraisal system a cutting edge. You had to be able to distinguish between the outstanding and the average, or else, in the earlier 'pseudo-socialist' way of disbursing rewards, the exceptional performers would be demotivated and feel there was really no point putting in the extra effort. All that changed swiftly; high-performers could chart a career path or a markedly different trajectory.

Naik says that in every project and plan, he first looks for the leaders. They are a make-or-break factor because time and again they have the ability to make people perform to peak potential. Naik has translated his thoughts about leadership into action, and to witness action in the leadership development domain, we journeyed around 100 kilometres from the city of Mumbai to Lonavala, in the foothills of the Western Ghats.

# A.M. Naik

## Idyllic ambience

As we walked up towards its cafeteria, past manicured lawns and a golf course, we couldn't help thinking that the L&T Leadership Development Academy (LDA) looked more like a hill resort for the affluent than a corporate learning centre. The buildings ebb and flow with the contours of the landscape, and the manicured trees and lawns add to the natural greenery and beauty of the area. Inside, however, was a different story—elaborate learning halls, discussion rooms, tele-conferencing facilities and a well-stocked library. It was a place to learn, un-learn and re-learn.

The LDA is a residential facility, and we were told that employees looked forward to opportunities to enrol in courses. Though the institution actually predates Naik taking over the reins, it had led a quiet existence. But when Naik visited the campus, he looked at it through the lens of the future, for he is an inveterate builder of 'tomorrow' at every level. He unfurled a new future for the LDA, expanding it more than twice over, and embellishing it. It became an institute that could live up to its advertising slogan—'A place to mould the minds that mould the future'. It is at this institution that L&T's talent from all levels— trainees to top management—converge periodically.

Spotting talent, fostering it and retaining it is Naik's passion. He also inducted a clutch of management consultancies for different aspects of L&T's operations, to provide the external perspective on all the change that he was contemplating.

Like 'constant value addition', Naik also introduced the term 'global benchmarking'. Being the best in India was no longer enough; L&T had to be as good as, if not better than, the best in the world. Most employees would not have realized it then, but Naik was getting the company ready for a world where national boundaries were getting blurred. While many have touched on this aspect, it was M.V. Kotwal, former director on the L&T board, who expressed it with succinct clarity.

'Of all the things that Naik gave to this organization, the single most important is the ability to look at oneself through an international lens. Consider where the world has gone, and see for yourself where you stand on the global stage,' Kotwal said. In other words, wake up and smell the coffee. Even the most ambitious of professionals can tend to become complacent when they know there is no serious competition. What Naik did was expand the universe for L&T employees—not India, not Asia, but the world.

Kotwal recalled that the share of L&T's heavy engineering in global markets was not significant. 'I know for a fact that in engineering, our international business was very small. Naik came in and gave it a completely different colour. That outside-in approach, the way of looking at things from a global level, is his permanent contribution to this organization,' he said.

Naik set about institutionalizing a process where every phase and system of the company's operations—from project engineering through product manufacture to customer support—was appraised against global benchmarks. The results are apparent in the scale, sophistication and speed that now characterize L&T's projects. The company has built the world's biggest reactors, longest bridges, finest airport terminals and most complex refineries; and all of them have been completed within stringent schedules, matching global standards.

# A.M. Naik

## Consummate communicator

Change of such magnitude, across a large, widely dispersed organization, needs to be fuelled by continuous and powerful communication with all stakeholders. In Naik, the company found a consummate communicator, a captivating speaker blessed with a booming voice and the ability to weave multiple arguments together. Soon after Naik took over as CEO in 1999, he went on a tour of L&T's sprawling campuses across the country to muster enthusiasm among employees. He addressed scores of meetings, speaking at times for over an hour. The mission was critical: how do you make a large, multi-locational organization think, feel and act like one?

Naik's method was simple and effective. Where there was doubt and uncertainty, he offered clarity; where there was a multiplicity of the opinion, he presented a single, unifying stance; most importantly, he won hearts and minds of his audience. He was shaping the future of the organization. That is probably why R. Gopalakrishnan and Pallavi Mody described Naik as a 'shaper'—an achiever of a higher order than a 'leader'—in their book *How Anil Naik Built L&T's Remarkable Growth Trajectory*.

In addition, Naik sent out a number of letters to employees. It is always encouraging to receive a letter signed by the CEO, as it indicates that the employee isn't just expected to follow orders but is being made privy to the transformation process. One of Naik's first letters informed employees about what to expect in the days to come. Every missive was like a missile, disrupting the surroundings and sending out ripples of change.

## The New L&T

Here is an excerpt from a July 1999 letter announcing a task force:

> The L&T task force members will be responsible for coordinating internally and providing detailed data required to evaluate the main businesses (today and future), corporate and business unit organization structure and existing value-based management processes, e.g. MIS (management information systems), incentive compensation, etc. These task force members will also provide an internal qualitative perspective to assess any current shortcomings/weaknesses along the above dimensions. They will also act as an active thought partner with the global management consultancy firm Boston Consultancy Group (BCG) in generating recommendations for improvements. Each task force will be led by a 'champion' who will facilitate the team process to achieve maximum gains. The task force champions, whenever required, will invite some of you to their meetings.
>
> The BCG team members will be primarily responsible for testing the key assumptions underlying the L&T strategic plans, and provide an external perspective on the best practices across key value-creation dimensions. They will also act as an active thought partner, with the L&T task forces, in generating recommendations for the company to become a premier conglomerate.

The last sentence of the letter is of special relevance: 'This is one of the most important transformation efforts that we have embarked upon, and I request your active participation and contribution, which will go a long way in making L&T a world leader.'

The target was steep. Naik was not saying that L&T would become a world leader immediately but that the contribution of employees would 'go a long way' towards it. It was a clear case of high expectations balanced by pragmatism. The message that was sent out was that L&T will have to change. What did the change involve? The short answer is just about everything—what the company does, how it does so and who would make the change.

Naik had already taken the first step up the value chain. It would soon be followed by another, then another and then another. Soon, the company would end up at a place where few had gone before. In an interview, Naik explained exactly what it takes to build a new company—it is not just vision, it is the nuts and bolts.

As part of the process of making the new L&T more entrepreneurially oriented, Naik rewrote the established ways things were done. In the specific field of heavy engineering, here are excerpts from a report where he explained the changes he had brought about: 'We dropped carbon steel and stainless steel. We brought in alloy steel and very advanced fabrication material. Then, we went on increasing the thickness of metal. We moved up from 50 mm; now we are largely in the 100 mm thick zone, with different materials, applications and industries. The number of players in India is minuscule; in fact, the number of players around the world is also very small. Obviously, your competition becomes a little less when you go higher up the tree. You then get a higher price.'

We had not heard of a simpler, sharper explanation of how you ascend the value chain in heavy engineering.

# The New L&T

## A technology-driven tomorrow

Around that time, Naik articulated for the first time an IT Vision for the company. The company had been taking baby steps into the IT domain, when Naik took over at the helm. But a major problem L&T encountered was persistently high levels of attrition. L&T had begun implementing the enterprise resource software SAP, and engineers who gained expertise in SAP suddenly became hot property across the industry, within India and even more so abroad. As the old saying goes, if you can't beat them, join them. Naik figured the best way to retain talent was to become a full-fledged IT company. In any case, at the back of his mind, Naik knew that the future belonged to IT.

## Entrepreneurial inputs

You can see Naik's signature style in the transformation across all of L&T's businesses. Take construction as an example—one of L&T's oldest businesses. It was only after 2006 that construction began to be more closely integrated with the rest of the company, so that it could scale up everything it did. The results were spectacular. In just eleven years post 2006, the infrastructure business grew around twenty times and profits zoomed forty-five times.

## Beyond boundaries

The company's emphasis on exports took both Brand L&T and Brand India beyond domestic shores. This involved not just a change in markets but also a change in mindset. The company began to establish its footprint across geographies, and overseas revenues today account for nearly one-third of its total turnover. All this is the outcome of the international thrust initiated in 2000.

## Nation-building

Alongside value creation for shareholders, Naik never lost sight of the overarching goal—L&T was here to serve the nation. Today, the company is recognized as a nation-builder and private-sector partner in the strategic areas of defence, nuclear power and aerospace. L&T has for long been a barometer of national development, and its stock is a surrogate for infrastructure. While L&T has always been known to actively participate in nation-building (that was what drew the young Naik to the company in the first place), after he took over at the helm, he aligned L&T more closely to national priorities. More on this in the next chapter, 'India First, India Always'.

It's not just the projects they build, it's the song they sing—the L&T anthem is a paean to the nation. Unlike other corporate anthems which are unabashedly self-congratulatory, the L&T anthem talks instead of redeeming the debt they owe to the land they were born in. Stirring stuff!

## Institutions of learning

We have already spoken about the iconic Leadership Development Academy in Lonavala. There is also an Institute of Project Management, with campuses in Vadodara and Chennai. In his foreword to the institute's brochure, Naik wrote: 'Projects are the engines that drive innovation from idea to commercialization. Projects are also the drivers that make organizations better, stronger, and more efficient.' The stated mission of the institute is to integrate itself with the practising project manager to create and disseminate project management learnings for future project managers.

Then there is L&T's 7-Step Leadership Programme, a structured process that identifies and incubates leaders. This programme provides exposure to the crème de la crème of global business schools, culminating in personal mentoring by Naik. So there are potential leaders waiting in the wings to take the company forward into the future. HR departments like to call this a 'leadership pipeline', and in L&T's case, Naik has ensured that the pipeline shows no sign of drying up.

**Values are sacrosanct**

While Naik brought about a lot of changes, there were some things he left exactly as they were; these were sacrosanct. In all the scramble for market share and push for profits, Naik knew that businesses would face a dilemma—should they compromise on values or miss out on a lucrative opportunity? Naik stayed firm; for him, the core values of the organization were inviolable. No cutting corners, no questionable practices; you simply play by the rules.

As Naik himself put it in an interview: 'The company's remarkable growth has been achieved without deviating at any stage from its core values.'

The new L&T is adept at swiftly pushing back goal posts. What does one do after achieving one's goal? You might say, 'One basks in the glow of achievement, of course.' Naik does not indulge in this luxury. At the customary function to mark the completion of a project, Naik's eyes inevitably turn to the next target, a bigger and more complex challenge. It is by constantly raising the bar that he has been able to sustain his soaring record of achievements—raising value, enhancing talent, elevating levels of productivity and remaining on the frontline of a constantly evolving business.

A compelling leader sets a behavioural template for the rest of the team, and those working under Naik soon realize the need to eradicate complacence. He also raises the bar when it comes to scale. It might appear safe to settle for the small and aim to proceed in incremental steps, but he can never be content with this timid approach. He is unafraid to unfurl the wide canvas of ambition and thinks scale even when constrained by circumstance. When the rest of the company used to talk about projects worth about ₹10 crore or thereabouts, he would shake up them all up with a target of ₹50 crore or ₹100 crore. Now, the targets are even higher—always over a thousand crore. Thinking scale has enabled Naik to develop a series of businesses that today contribute more than a billion dollars to revenue. When he sets such high benchmarks, he widens the horizons of all those he influences down the line. Soon, everyone in the team is thinking scale.

Naik's footprint is all across the L&T network in India and overseas. 'Tomorrow' is writ large across the facilities built in his time. Apart from his eponymous facility in Hazira, about which a local magazine enthusiastically said 'he found it a marsh, he left it a marvel', there are several others. Closest is Knowledge City in Vadodara. Naik believes that manufacturing and design should be at the proverbial arm's length distance, and Vadodara fit the bill. So if Hazira is the muscle of L&T, Knowledge City is its mind—and what a mind! Masterfully designed, the complex provides the stimulating environment to keep design and engineering minds ticking and IT-related projects buzzing. Naik also set up facilities for a slew of new-age businesses in and around Coimbatore, Bengaluru and Mysuru. The vast sweep of Kattupalli in Tamil Nadu may still not have gained full maturity, but there is certainly an upside to this facility that stands on the shores of Bay of Bengal. Each of these locations has its own 'Naik story' to tell, perhaps biding its time and its own book.

## Succession planning

Another process that has changed dramatically is succession planning. The disquieting uncertainty that used to prevail when it was time for leadership to change hands earlier was replaced by the comforting assurance that only a structured process brings. The leadership transition that took place in L&T in September 2023 ranks among the smoothest corporate successions in Indian industry. His successor-to-be, S.N. Subrahmanyan was identified, groomed and personally mentored by Naik, as are most members of L&T's current leadership team. Characteristically thinking ahead of time, he engaged with around twenty-five top executives to ensure that L&T has leadership visibility for as far as 2040.

It is obvious that the new L&T puts in longer hours and works harder than before. This could appear to be in conflict with the thinking of young people today, with their new-found fetish for 'work-life balance'. Frankly, we do not believe that either life or work can be measured by the time you spend—that is like measuring happiness by the kilo! What really matters is how much you truly enjoy what you are doing.

Naik's working style has set a trend within the organization; many others in the company have tried to emulate him. They may not be able to sustain the long hours, but in their own way, they too try to achieve a different interpretation of work-life balance.

---

On 15 March 2024, Naik received the ET Lifetime Achievement Award at the hands of the External Affairs Minister S. Jaishankar. He dedicated the award to his late father. In his acceptance speech, delivered to an audience which included the Finance Minister Nirmala Sitharaman, and a host of luminaries from across the administration and industry, he carried a message that, we believe, is of particular relevance to India's citizens. Naik highlighted the contrast between his humble beginnings as a schoolmaster's son and his meteoric rise in the corporate world. As he likes to put it, it was an event-studded journey—from a village to the world. It was an achievement that should act as inspiration to young men and women across the land. Here are excerpts from his acceptance speech.

> Being conferred with The Economic Times Lifetime Achievement Award is a milestone moment for me and a

signal honour for the company to which I have devoted my life—Larsen & Toubro ...

To me, awards are an affirmation not just of what an individual has achieved but also what he or she believes in. My life's ambition all along has been to participate in the grand journey of building the nation in whatever way I could. I am happy that this mission has found resonance with Larsen & Toubro—so much so that L&T is widely acknowledged as a barometer of national growth.

All this could not have happened at a more opportune time. Under the leadership of the Prime Minister and his able team—some of whom are present here—we are poised on a historic threshold to move closer to our goal of building a strong nation and a vibrant and inclusive society. Of all the things that our Prime Minister has done, I believe the most important is that he has instilled in us the courage to believe in our dreams and given us the power to make our dreams real.

Let me conclude with a personal message: it is unreasonable to expect the government alone to take exclusive responsibility for our collective aspirations. Each of us can lend a hand. Together we will get to our goals faster.

In many ways, the new L&T resembles the new India around us today—more self-assured, assertive, impatient and decisive. Naik has thus moulded the company to faithfully mirror many of his personal characteristics. We have every reason to believe this will set the template for tomorrow, because Naik has chosen his successor wisely—Subrahmanyan shares many of Naik's more striking qualities.

We have titled this chapter 'The New L&T' because in time, Subrahmanyan will build further on the platform set up by Naik and realize his own distinct vision of another 'new L&T', which will help it scale greater heights. Company historians tell us L&T never remains static; it is always reinventing itself while keeping its core values sacrosanct. Fortunately, at crucial junctures, it has always found the right leader at the helm. Today, that helmsman is Subrahmanyan. He has picked up the baton and is racing towards the future. Tomorrow, here we come.

# 5

# India First, India Always

*'Think of any of the names that strike a chord with people—* *INS* *Arihant, K9 Vajra, Chandrayaan, Mangalyaan, the Statue of Unity, the Ram Temple ... L&T has been engaged with them all.'*

NAIK WEARS HIS NATIONALISM ON HIS SLEEVE—OR RATHER, ON HIS lapel, where a tiny metal tricolour remains pinned. We also see a large flag made of fabric—more than one, sometimes—fluttering in all of L&T's campuses and offices around the world.

'I am very proud of being an Indian, so I carry this Indian flag wherever I go. It reminds me of my duty to the nation at every moment,' he said.

This is even more apparent in his activities and decisions. When filmmaker Zafar Hai asked him what nationalism meant to him, Naik said: 'Nationalism means action.'

If we read between the lines of his comment, 'nationalism' is not chest-thumping, not jingoistic catchphrases or hollow ranting; it is simply believing, thinking and doing what is right by your country. We have rarely come across a deeper and more level-headed definition of the word. Naik has for long demonstrated this meaningful kind of nationalism. It could well be in his genes—his father was part of the freedom struggle.

As we have already said before, the young Anil was very clear about his career path. His ideal job would involve engineering (after all, he has been trained as an engineer). And the company he would work for should be contributing in one way or another to the grand process of nation-building. Destiny and perseverance brought him to his dream career destination. Decades later, when he took over the reins of the company and was in a position to influence its course, he aligned L&T more closely with the most vital needs of the nation. These included the strategic areas of defence, nuclear power and aerospace, as well as complex infrastructure—all of which earned it the sobriquet 'builder to the nation'.

But there is something less visible and possibly more important. Naik is not just a patriot; he evokes patriotism in others. He has led the kind of life that helped remould people's mindsets. We have come across many Indians with a curious diffidence about expressing patriotism—it is as if they would be happier if they had been born in some other country far, far away. We must confess we ourselves are occasionally guilty of harbouring a slight sense of inferiority when comparing India with the world's advanced nations. Naik would have none of it; he instils pride and a heightened, possibly more accurate, awareness of country and community. He made it 'cool' to be Indian.

## Rejigging the compass

In the 1980s and 1990s, there was an unspoken but unshakeable assumption that in the world of high technology, the sun rose in the West—large and complex industrial equipment could only be manufactured there and then shipped to the East. Then came Hazira and other large manufacturing complexes—'growth centres', as Nayak would call them—around India.

Naik had rejigged the compass, and the results began to show. Equipment made of exotic metals and with complex names—hydrocracking reactors, polypropylene reactors, ethylene oxide reactors, coal gasifiers—began to sail from India to the world.

Post the 1990s, whenever clean fuel programmes were implemented in the US, Canada or Europe, almost 90 per cent of the fuel was processed through L&T reactors.

## Leap into space

To understand how these winds of change are sweeping across India's strategic sectors, we need to turn our eyes away from terrestrial objects and gaze skywards—to the moon, Mars and the sun. Larsen & Toubro has been involved in India's space odyssey—from development of boosters for the launch vehicle for the maiden journey four-and-a-half decades back. Unstinted encouragement every step of the subsequent way came from Naik and others in senior leadership. In Chandrayaan-3, for example, L&T provided critical, high-tech systems for which multiple facilities pitched in. The range was wide—from the manufacture of subsystems for the vehicle itself to tracking its path all along its celestial route.

Getting into the details involves technical nitty-gritty: critical booster segments (head-end and middle) and the nozzle bucket flange were manufactured and proof pressure tested at Powai. Ground and flight umbilical plates were manufactured at L&T's high-tech facility in Coimbatore, which is specifically meant for aerospace manufacturing. The L&T-made Precision Monopulse Tracking Radar at the Satish Dhawan Space Centre in Sriharikota is used to track the early part of the ascent of the launch vehicles. The company has also commissioned the Deep Space Network antenna in Byalalu, a village in Karnataka just an hour's drive from Bengaluru, which enabled India's space scientists track the Chandrayaan's ascent and bring data to mission control centre.

Naik joined many of his fellow Indians in watching intently and applauding enthusiastically as the rover Pragyan touched down on the moon's surface. But Chandrayaan-3 is only one among many recent milestones in L&T's association with India's space mission—the company was right there when the first Satellite Launch Vehicle (SLV-3) soared into the skies above Sriharikota in 1979, and since then, it has been an unfailing part of every space mission, from small steps to giant leaps.

This augurs well for L&T's future—the space sector is just about to open its doors to Indian industry, and this company in particular can leverage its long association with the Indian Space Research Organisation to play a bigger role.

Soon one day, the country will send Indians into orbit, and L&T will be part of that programme too. L&T will be part of both the unmanned as well as the crewed missions. L&T has already delivered the first human-rated motor case hardware for the mission in 2020 and has built a crew capsule. More will follow as India takes epoch-making steps towards its destiny in space.

**Defence of the nation**

You don't need guns only to win wars. You need them to deter your enemies and win peace. Defence is another strategic sector that bears Naik's distinctive imprint. To understand its contours better, we travelled to Kattupalli, less than thirty kilometres north of Chennai. This complex is both incubator and nursery of some of the most advanced vessels being made by L&T. The campus encompasses a fabrication yard for oil and gas projects, but the prime focus now is on vessels for defence. The list is long: frigates, destroyers, corvettes and Offshore Patrol Vessels. In addition to 'new-builds', as the industry refers to them, the yard also undertakes high-tech ship repair and service. It made headlines in 2023 when the US Navy and L&T entered into a Master Ship Repair Agreement. Multiple American vessels have since docked at the facility for voyage repairs.

Kattupalli was yet another brainchild of Naik's, and one can tell it has been set up by a man engaged in building for tomorrow. The campus is large—a thousand acres. A lot can happen here once the Government of India is more receptive to involving the private sector in defence manufacture.

It was Naik's nationalistic dream that L&T would be the first private company to be taken on board by the Indian Navy, especially for its strategic programme. A retired admiral who also worked for L&T had warm words of praise. 'You can imagine the vision of Mr Naik,' he said. 'We built the blocks at Hazira, took them by barge all the way to Visakhapatnam, loaded them onto the dock and then joined them together, and the submarine would finally get its shape.'

Being involved in the nation's strategic programme is understandably very prestigious, but your bragging rights are curtailed. Much of your involvement remains, for obvious reasons, under wraps, bound by tight secrecy norms. This rigorous application of confidentiality rules became most apparent when L&T's engineers were involved in making what could be called one of the Indian Navy's most hush-hush projects ever—INS *Arihant*, India's maiden nuclear-powered submarine. Until it was officially announced on 26 July 2009, it was never even referred to as a submarine. Not many in L&T knew what was happening. Only a few, including those in the corporate communications department, were brought into the inner circle, tasked with creating an advertisement but unable to talk freely about it. Cryptically, the submarine was only referred to as 'the object'. The veil of secrecy was finally lifted when a large advertisement appeared in *The Times of India* and other national publications, talking about how L&T had helped the Indian Navy do what few navies have done.

Naik was among the select group invited to witness the launch of INS *Arihant* in Visakhapatnam, on the anniversary of India's military victory at Kargil. Among those present were then-PM Manmohan Singh, then-defence minister A.K. Antony and a virtual who's who of the Indian defence sector. Television reports showed Naik in his element, shaking hands effusively with admirals, generals and officials, while undoubtedly pressing home the point that L&T had been closely involved with this prestigious national project.

Most people are reticent to talk about what L&T does to guard the nation. The affable and articulate J.D. Patil, currently adviser to the chairman and managing director, and A.V. Parab, executive director on the L&T board, talk in general terms about 'our' capabilities, rather than telling you specifically about what L&T has done. However, both are more forthcoming about how Naik was an unfailing source of encouragement in their efforts.

Defence is not FMCG—the wheels at South Block move slowly, and patience and perseverance are vital if you want to stay the course. Just one illustrative example will suffice: the submarine programme, which started in the mid-1980s, only got into 'build phase' in the late 1990s. Naik understood well the constraints that L&T's defence team was working under. He knew that was how this game was played, and provided constant reassurance.

The army is as bound with confidentiality clauses as the navy and the air force. So there is a lot that we must not talk about. But among the highlights that have made it to the public domain is the K9 Vajra-T, the howitzer that carries an air of well-groomed menace. It can throw longer punches than the other famed battle-equipment-on-tracks—the tank—and does not need line of sight, meaning you can hit an unseen enemy who's cowering behind a hill. Also, the howitzer belongs to the artillery, and in the words attributed to the legendary American general of World War II George S. Patton: 'I don't need to tell you who won the war. You know the artillery did.'

Modern weapons incorporate a lot of technology and gadgetry. We can all see for ourselves that technology is changing the way we work, earn a living, entertain ourselves and lead our daily lives. Less happily, technology is also changing the way we fight. Pacifists may turn around and tell us there ought to be no wars. Ideally, yes, but history is a harsh teacher and tells us that conflicts are bound to crop up when our self-interests collide with the interests of our neighbours. When peace initiatives flounder and there seems to be nothing to be gained by turning the other cheek, war becomes the only solution left. It then makes eminent practical sense to be prepared. As US President Theodore Roosevelt said: 'Speak softly and carry a big stick.'

The 'stick' that tomorrow's combatants will carry will look a lot different from today's. Future battlefields could be far removed from the frontiers and soldiers may not need to squeeze a trigger; they will only need to tap a key. And L&T is geared for it—Naik's patient and unstinted encouragement has made sure that L&T's defence engineering capabilities are future ready.

To learn more about L&T's prowess, we visited the Aero India air show in Bengaluru. The roar of planes streaking across the noonday sky and a display of *Top Gun*-style aerobatics always bring visitors to their feet.

On the ground, though, there are more prosaic but possibly more meaningful interactions between the military brass and manufacturers of defence equipment and systems. Larsen & Toubro's presence was highlighted through its collaboration with MBDA, the Paris-headquartered developer and manufacturer of missiles. Among the key attractions at the stall was the indigenously designed and manufactured fifth-generation anti-tank guided missile system. Also on display was the latest-generation naval air defence weapons system, christened VL-SRSAM, which protects the host platform and escorts shipping for around twenty-five kilometres.

## Infrastructure underpins progress

The words of much-loved former PM Atal Bihari Vajpayee echo through our minds: 'This is another of the things that L&T makes that makes India proud.'

Rarely, if ever, does a Prime Minister quote a private company's advertising tag line. But when it comes to its association with the nation, L&T is treated as rather special.

Vajpayee spoke these words at a grand function on 22 November 1998 to inaugurate HITEC City—L&T's software park in a section of Hyderabad that has since come to be known as Cyberabad.

Since then, many heads of the national government and many more heads of state governments have inaugurated major projects built by L&T—such as the aforementioned Statue of Unity and the Narendra Modi Stadium in Ahmedabad, plus metro systems in many state capitals, the Mumbai Trans Harbour Link—India's longest sea bridge and the precedent-setting coastal road in Mumbai. Nobody can deny that in all cases, the projects ranked as exceptional, the kind that make every Indian proud.

Infrastructure was one of L&T's earliest businesses. In fact, in technical terms, it is even older than L&T, having been set up as a private limited company in 1944, when L&T was still a partnership.

The canvas of construction is vast—much wider than, say, heavy engineering or hydrocarbon projects—but its growth remained somewhat muted until Naik took over the reins and brought the construction business in line with the other businesses. Then things changed with scaling up of projects and rapid growth of profits. So strongly is L&T identified with building national assets that *The Economic Times* once captioned a picture of Naik as 'Mr Infrastructure'. Even more interesting is the story of how he once paid a visit to the home of a large family-owned corporation that developed major hydropower and cement projects across the country.

Naik was greeted warmly by the family scion. 'Mr Naik,' said the young man, 'my father calls you the Amitabh Bachchan of infrastructure.'

Naik responded instantaneously: 'In that case, your father is Dilip Kumar and you are Shah Rukh Khan.'

## When the Buddha smiled

On 18 May 1974, the private phone in PM Indira Gandhi's office rang briefly; she picked it up to hear the eagerly awaited words: 'The Buddha has smiled.'

## India First, India Always

It is probably India's best remembered code. It meant that India's first test of its nuclear capabilities, conducted in Pokhran on the day of Buddha Purnima, had been successful. The smile lit up India's path to a new nuclear future, with lasting long-term implications. We became a de-facto member of the elite Nuclear Club.

Not everybody was smiling—across the world in Canada, consternation reigned. How could a 'third world' country do it, they asked in righteous indignation. How could India have the temerity to test a device when the Canadians were officially assisting us to build nuclear reactors solely for the generation of nuclear power? Apart from the fact that the zealously guarded nuclear formula of the US and Canada was out, we suspect that what got them terribly angry was that India had made them all look rather foolish.

Retribution was swift. Canada and the US both pulled out their nuclear engineers from India and suspended their assistance programmes. Seeing this, the rest of the world pulled out too. They thought that bereft of international assistance, India's nuclear ambitions in the civilian sector—and thus the military sector too—would be stillborn. Enter L&T and its manufacturing capabilities. Independent engineers say that there was virtually nothing to distinguish India's first indigenous nuclear reactor built by L&T from the best of foreign-made reactors. Since then, L&T has since been involved in manufacturing almost all the nuclear reactors made in India. In addition to engineering equipment, L&T also builds critical civil structures, including those massive domes characteristic of nuclear power plants.

Naik is closely involved in fostering L&T's association with national missions. The company has an excellent equation with ISRO for space, the Defence Research and Development Organisation (DRDO) for defence equipment, and with the Nuclear Power Corporation of India. It's all part of a vision of making L&T a partner to major national endeavours.

## Equations with national leadership

So fervent is Naik's espousal of national causes that he corresponds with top leaders, offering encouragement and counsel at almost every critical juncture. In 2008, when India managed to secure the contentious nuclear waiver from the US, he promptly shot off a letter to PM Manmohan Singh.

> Respected Dr Manmohan Singhji,
>
> Please accept our congratulations for the outstanding success achieved by you in securing the NSG waiver.
>
> We applaud you on your strong leadership, dedication to the nation, and perseverance, because of which this signal success has been achieved. We believe this is a major step towards realization of your vision of putting India at her rightful position in the world, and wish you even more success.
>
> At L&T, we are particularly happy to see one more opportunity to contribute to the building of the nation, and we recommit ourselves to that task.
>
> Yours sincerely,
> A.M. Naik.

## India First, India Always

On another occasion, and with another Prime Minister, Naik's flow of correspondence continues: after the G20 Summit in New Delhi in September 2023, Naik wrote to PM Narendra Modi.

> Every Indian today stands an inch taller than ever before. And it is all thanks to the marvellous work that you are doing for the country on key fronts.
>
> Brand Bharat, under your leadership, is gradually taking its rightful place in the global community. Just two days ago, we witnessed the conclusion of the most successful G20 to date. The Delhi Declaration can truly be said to be a triumph of your transcending vision and your ability to bridge international differences and steer the world towards shared goals of global growth and prosperity.
>
> In addition to joining the international chorus of felicitations for G20, let me add my commendations for your masterful manner in which you have led the nation's economy. Thanks to the number of positive decisions taken by your government, the Indian economy today is an oasis of stability amid global uncertainty. I am sure that we are collectively taking rapid strides towards the inspirational USD 5 trillion goal that you have set.
>
> On the domestic front, I wholeheartedly commend the 'One Nation, One Election Bill' that your government plans to introduce soon. This is an electoral reform that the country ought to have introduced decades ago. Apart from helping the country by effecting enormous savings, it will

eliminate disruptions caused by multiple election cycles, and enable your government to get out of perpetual campaign mode and devote more time and energy on advancing the country's growth agenda.

A.M. Naik

And it's not always kind words and praise; Naik is equally forthright when there are problems that need to be tackled. He frequently talks to government officials, such as the cabinet secretary, outlining problems and offering solutions. 'Change is needed on many fronts and at many levels, and I would be happy to help make it happen,' he says. His words carry weight in the corridors of power as they come from an obviously transparent nationalist.

More home truths, politely but emphatically told, lay in an article contributed by Naik in early 2022 for Bloomberg Quint (BQ Prime). The magazine had asked industry leaders for their wish list—all that they expect from policymakers. Naik, being Naik, did not mince words:

> Uncertainty and discontinuity are a recurring nightmare for business planners. The renewable energy sector, for instance, has seen state governments reneging with impunity on existing PPAs in a bid to secure power at recently discovered low prices. This negatively impacts IRRs of current investments and puts a damper on future investment. It is also becoming increasingly clear that India's outmoded dispute resolution and arbitration processes need to be brought in tune with

current needs. Already overburdened with a backlog of cases, our country's legal system seems ill-equipped to handle another avalanche—arbitration cases. It needs to be appreciated that all investments are based on certain projections of demand, traffic, off-take, etc. Such carefully made plans are thrown out of gear when major deviations are undertaken after the project or asset gets operational. For the authorities, the arbitration route seems the easy way out—with adverse consequences for hapless investors.

In continuation to this point, it would be helpful if our infrastructure planners step back and look at the big picture. Piecemeal planning and myopic implementation of projects lead to unaddressed gaps, thereby impacting demand, traffic and flow. While attempts have been made to address this through the Gati Shakti programme, it is obvious that it may not be enough. In a federal economy like India, such programmes and their acceptance need to percolate to the levels of the urban local bodies, municipal corporations, etc.

No wish list of any investor worth the name will end without the fervent desire to cut down bureaucratic red tape and expediting governance processes. The implementation of single-window clearance can be prioritized, particularly in case of environmental clearances, mining permissions, etc. States and municipal bodies could also be incentivized to integrate into this system so that investors do not run into unexpected local issues. Even government departments responsible for clearances ought to draw up service-level agreements. Would it not be wonderful if delays and deviations from stated timelines meant automatic approval!

Years ago, the magazine *Business Today* quoted Naik as saying: 'When it comes to L&T, everyone speaks their heart out. They know we aren't working for our own self-interest, but are nation-builders. That's the reason top political leaders classify L&T as the only national sector company.'

The high esteem in which political leaders regard L&T cuts across party lines. At the launch of the nuclear-powered submarine INS *Arihant* at Visakhapatnam, PM Manmohan Singh had told him: 'Truly, Mr Naik, you have a company you can be proud about.'

The sentiment is widely shared by many in the country's leadership circles. J.D. Patil recounts: 'Dr A.P.J. Abdul Kalam believed that L&T could solve any challenge in technology development. So when he moved into defence research, he told Mr Naik that he would need a lot of help on the missile programme. We, of course, responded positively. We told him, "Tell us what you want, and will produce it." It turned out to be a success at the national level. And all through, Mr Naik did not look over his employees' shoulders. He left you to do what you do best, and he would keep a watch.'

**Evangelizing patriotism**

Naik's overriding passion for nation-building is widely recognized by the country's institutions of learning. The Indian Institute of Management, Lucknow, was eloquent in profiling his accomplishments: 'Mr A. Naik is the visible face and eloquent spokesperson not only of the company he heads but of the Indian manufacturing sector. He has the visionary's ability to see beyond immediate horizons, and the industrialist's capability to engineer change. Through precept, practice and passionate advocacy, he evokes in the youth a zeal to follow his cause of nation-building.'

As we said earlier, Naik evangelizes patriotism. He drives home the message of serving the nation at virtually every opportunity—at industry forums and academic institutions. He is flooded with requests from major national institutes and accepts as many as he can fit into his calendar. His central message is largely the same—he does not tell the young graduates what they would like to hear but what he believes they ought to know. In 2023, for example, he told the students graduating from IIM Ahmedabad a few home truths.

'Some of you may have already firmed up your plans to accept lucrative offers from overseas. I would urge you to pause and reflect on what you are doing. We all have a larger obligation towards our homeland, the nation which has made us what we are. You are the brightest talents of our country, and you have the responsibility of helping India realize its vision,' Naik said.

He added that remaining in the country would not interfere with their professional goals. 'I can assure you that you will find enough opportunity in India to challenge your capabilities and fulfil your aspirations. You will get a sense of satisfaction you will never get anywhere abroad.'

A decade ago, there are those who could have questioned Naik on why his own son, Jignesh, had chosen to look for greener pastures in the US. After all, if charity begins at home, so must patriotism. But today, nobody can point a finger at him—Jignesh has retraced his steps; he has come back home. Beaming with pride, Naik told us that in an environment where most young people would jump at the first opportunity to claim American citizenship, only one in a thousand would still hold on to the Indian passport.

**Speaking truth to power**

As we have said before, Naik's deep, abiding love for the country does not stop him from pointing out its shortcomings, and there are many of them. They are the outcome of myopic policy roadmaps, short-term thinking and, to call a spade a spade, political expediency. He has repeatedly urged industry and the government to work unitedly for the benefit of the nation and its people. He is certainly impressed with India's achievements in recent years, but this does not blind him to the many problems that the country faces. Sometimes after a public euphoria has been generated, it makes sense to get a reality check. 'Ours is a very poor country,' Naik says with candour. And while he may not quite subscribe to the findings of the World Hunger Index, which controversially ranked India 111 among 125 countries, he is realistic enough to acknowledge that there is a lot to be done.

In an annual address to shareholders, Naik did not pussyfoot around the inequalities and income disparities that blight our country's progress.

'There cannot be an India for the rich, and an India for the rest. Unity in diversity is commendable, but unity in disparity is fraught with risks. And even if the country were somehow able to accommodate such imbalances, it will be unacceptable to anyone with a social conscience,' he said.

Publications frequently ask him to write for their special editions on the Indian nation. Naik wrote one of these for *Businessworld* on the seventieth anniversary of India's independence in 2017, making several pertinent points that deserve a wider audience, and we take the liberty of reproducing extensive excerpts.

> We have come a long way from 1947. We have endured, and indeed thrived. We are the only functioning democracy in our neighbourhood, and this is entirely due to the people of this country who have kept faith in the democratic process.
>
> But we still have a long way to go to be reckoned as an economic powerhouse. While absolute numbers might give us some comfort, the devil is in the details. Our GDP per capita puts us below at least a hundred other countries in the world. Our energy consumption per person is again below that of a hundred other countries.
>
> The difference is even starker in peer-to-peer comparisons. Countries like China and South Korea—almost on par with us in the 1950s—have left us far behind.
>
> When asked by *Businessworld* for my thoughts on turning India into an economic powerhouse, I felt the canvas was wide open. There are indeed a thousand things one can think of, which, if implemented efficiently, can get us to the goal. But for the purpose of this article, I will concentrate on the foremost issues.

*Mindset:* Historically, we have had a culture of not celebrating the successes of our fellow countrymen. Profit has always been looked down upon. It seems that making a profit is a crime, or that any profit made has been made by unfair means. We do not celebrate a Steve Jobs or an Elon Musk. Everywhere else in the developed world, success is something to be proud of. Countries hold their entrepreneurial successes as a beacon to attract talent from all over the world. We have to realize that talent flows to where it is appreciated. In India, the first aim of a businessman is to camouflage his success. Unless we bring success to the mainstream of public thought, we can only hope to become an economic success story.

*Technology:* Most of the skills we have trained our younger generation in may become obsolete in the next fifteen years. Various studies have estimated the impact of automation, robotics and Artificial Intelligence ... industry is making continuous efforts to increase the productivity of workers, which will further squeeze employment generation. Re-skilling our workforce for the economy of the automation era is the only way forward.

*Learning and re-learning:* A demographic dividend is not a guarantee of growth. Smaller countries have marched way past us in this area. To ensure that we are not left behind, we need to create world-class educational institutes. The IITs and IIMs were created serendipitously. However, they are not sufficient. A thorough review of our school and college syllabi is urgently required to prepare us for the new-age economy. While we have been cost-efficient copiers in the commoditized space of IT and pharma, we need to move up the value chain. And we need new centres of global learning excellence which will form the bedrock of this process.

*Natural resources:* It has been repeated ad nauseum that India possesses a wealth of natural resources. However, we have failed to exploit them efficiently. We have the capacity to be self-sufficient in almost every critical resource, except maybe oil. Green Revolution 2.0 is required to implement cutting-edge technologies such as drip irrigation, so that we can become a net food exporter. Our farm productivity is among the lowest in the world. Our farmers also need to be educated in soil investigation techniques, market forces and water utilization ... Indian industry is ready and is only looking for a favourable policy regime which will incentivize capacity addition and capital investment.

*Legal processes:* The time- and resource-consuming legal system in the country has been a great disincentive for new businesses to flourish. Every new businessman has been, at one point of time or the other, threatened with the legal stick. Arbitration procedures take forever, and industrial disputes are unresolved for longer than the disputants survive.

*Social equity:* No economic powerhouse can remain sustainable—or even be morally acceptable—unless it brings with it some measure of social equity. The Companies Act, 2013, which mandates corporate expenditure of 2 per cent of average PAT is well-intentioned, but not enough. Ultimately, legislation has its limits. There is within each of us a space which tells us to do something beyond the call of compulsion. I hope every Indian pays heed to that still, small voice.

*Climate of excellence:* Even if all the pieces in the jigsaw were to fall in place, we would still need a climate of excellence to hold them together. We would need, on part of all Indians, an uncompromising commitment to excellence, for 'chalta hai' [it's fine] is never going to get us where we want to go. Whether it is manufacturing or services, agriculture or AI, we need people who aim to be the best in the world, and [are] proud of what they do.

## Fighting the good fight

In trying to advance the interests of the nation, Naik is prepared to make enemies, often powerful ones. One cause that he took up in the late 1990s had to do with the duty on imported capital goods.

We were told the story by Narayanan Kumar, a non-executive director on L&T's board. Kumar was, at the time, part of the Confederation of Indian Industry (CII), and had a ringside view of the battle.

'Naik's battle was for L&T, but it was also a fight for the country. If you are allowed to import things free of duty, then jobs in India would be lost. Now, the people who favoured importing capital goods were very powerful and politically well-connected; they were giants,' he recalled.

## India First, India Always

'In Naik, however, domestic industry found a David who would gamely challenge the Goliaths. For Naik, this was a matter of principle. The companies he was so courageously opposing were also his clients, and he would have to work with them on other projects. But a principle is something you cannot flout.'

Naik believes that all of us, at some stage in our lives, need to go beyond narrow self-interest and, as his father had exhorted decades ago, 'think of others'. Members of a privileged elite cannot allow themselves to be insulated from the stark human condition around them. We know there are millions of our fellow citizens leading wretched lives, and we know their children go hungry each night. Just because we do not hear their cries doesn't mean they don't exist.

The harsh reality is that there is still a long way to go before we can honestly look ourselves in the mirror and say that we are building tomorrow's India, a more equitable, inclusive India, the India of a billion dreams.

That kind of sentiment can best be rounded up in the way we have seen Naik ending all his formal communications—with a rousing, resounding '*Jai Hind!*'

# 6
# IT—A Vision Vindicated

*'In an age of increasing technological parity, high-calibre talent is the differentiator between companies.'*

IN THE LONG CONFERENCE ROOM IN NAIK'S OFFICE IN MUMBAI'S PALI Hill, the mood turned upbeat. It was June 2019, and the three key figures seated around the table appeared pleased that a pivotal deal had been clinched. Naik was happy because this was another important milestone in realizing the IT vision that he had nurtured for decades. A smile lit up Subrahmanyan's face because with this acquisition, the IT cluster in L&T's portfolio could finally break into the big league. The third person in the room, coffee magnate V.G. Siddhartha, the dominant shareholder of the IT firm Mindtree, was also happy, but for different reasons—he was possibly hopeful that the deal he had just inked would help him tide over a financial crunch.

As it turned out, things did not work out well for Siddhartha. For reasons entirely unconnected with the deal that he had signed, Siddhartha seemed to have found himself in trouble. Events culminated in a tragedy that the Bangalore City Police later said was suicide. Neither Naik nor Subrahmanyan had any inkling of the unfortunate events that were about to unfold, culminating in what the police stated to be Mr Siddhartha's suicide. All they knew at the time was Siddhartha had offered them his stake in the IT company.

Most in the media had no idea of this meeting in Pali Hill and totally misread the entire sequence of events. They began calling it a 'hostile takeover'—a label that stuck for some time. On its part, L&T soon proceeded to take the acquisition to its logical conclusion. Except for a few hiccups caused by dispossessed promoters unable or unwilling to read the writing on the wall, the takeover went exactly as per plan.

On 14 November 2022, the two companies—L&T Infotech and Mindtree—came together in one of the largest mergers in the history of India's IT sector, as LTIMindtree. This new firm became the country's fifth-largest IT provider by market capitalization and sixth-largest by revenue. It would benefit from scale, allowing the company to pursue larger outsourcing contracts, as clients were increasingly looking to consolidate vendors in the challenging macro environment.

Addressing the media to unveil the prospects ahead, Naik said there was a lot to look forward to, that the new company, along with L&T Technology Services, would generate over USD 5.6 billion in

## IT—A Vision Vindicated

revenue. It would also help L&T in achieving its goal of increasing IT-enabled services to 25 per cent of the company's total business by 2026.

The entity, Naik said, is uniquely positioned to combine speed and scale by competing for larger deals, and offers greater ability to stick together for end-to-end offerings and deeper engagement with hyperscalers to generate significant value.

The most attractive thing about this merger, LTIMindtree head Debashis Chatterjee told Moneycontrol in October 2022, is that there is no overlap—LTI is very strong in terms of supply chain transformation, while Mindtree is the same for customer experience transformation. If you look at the strengths, they can really be complementary to each other, and will be only beneficial, he said.

The merger helped both companies in significant ways and continues to create value for stakeholders. LTIMindtree emerged as a digital powerhouse combining the engineering prowess of LTI and the experience capabilities of the erstwhile Mindtree. The perfect harmony of Mindtree's digital services and LTI's strong background in infrastructure management and enterprise applications equips LTIMindtree with a comprehensive suite of capabilities and solutions. This in turn would enable the company to live up to its tag line 'Get to the future faster'.

### Naik's secret sauce for the IT business

The IT story at L&T began soon after Naik took over the helm in 1999. As mentioned in a previous chapter, it began with a paradox—the company was winning orders but haemorrhaging talent, because engineers trained in the enterprise resource software SAP were being snapped up by other companies in alarming numbers. So dire was the situation that by the time the company found a replacement for one person, two more would have caught a flight to the US.

Naik decided a change of strategy was called for. If young engineers were leaving for greener pastures, well, he would set up the greenest pasture going. He decided to set up L&T's own IT company. An independent entity, LTI, so it could offer employees terms matching what the industry offered.

But even after forming this company, it was not roses all the way. Naik's new firm was a late entrant to the game, and in business, it is the early bird that gets the worm, so L&T had to contend with entrenched players who skilfully leveraged their historical advantage. There would have been times in the early years of LTI when Naik's faith in IT as the future was beginning to be questioned. He must have wondered if he had made the right move.

This is the make-or-break moment pioneers must face, when they decide to give up or soldier on. Naik obviously decided on the latter, redoubling his energy to make the IT business a success. He used to joke that in the beginning, he knew only one IT—income tax! From that time of professed ignorance, Naik has come a long way.

In those challenging early times, Naik had hand-picked K.R.L. Narasimhan as one of two individuals (the other being Sunil Pande) to lead the teams in the US.

## IT—A Vision Vindicated

'We [LTI] faced a lot of headwinds because business immediately after Y2K was hard to come by. It was Naik who kept our faith. We were fighting for a foothold on foreign territory, competing against entrenched players. Also, there was the matter of company culture—L&T had a different culture and mindset,' Narasimhan confessed.

On the plus side, there were just a few favourable points. The first was the Naik network—large, widely dispersed across different sectors and still not fully tapped. Second was the fact that Brand L&T was known and well-remembered among the Indian diaspora, and those who knew L&T would inevitably also have heard of its trailblazing head honcho. Finally, there was Naik's ability—one can almost say his trackrecord—to make the impossible possible. He had started from zero on the marshland of Hazira, in L&T's export thrust and in many other fields. He had started from zero before; he would do so again.

Sunil Pande recalled, 'After the year 2000, Naik took on personal responsibility for improving the IT business.' The general had come out to fight shoulder to shoulder with his troops and brought along a change of tactic.

'I have not seen a person with so much passion and dedication, doing such hard work and with such close involvement in the business. Naik was a man in a hurry. He wanted quick results,' added Pande.

It has happened time and again—Naik begins knowing next to nothing about a subject, he's curious to find out more, his extraordinarily rapid learning helps develop capabilities and, before you know it, he has mastered the game.

# A.M. Naik

## Every trick in the book

Gradually, LTI began to find its feet. Naik's hard-driving style made it difficult for his colleagues to keep pace, but it was delivering results.

He changed the trajectory of the team's business approach—he aimed for the top, the C-suite. He knew from experience that staff junior in their hierarchy would not be able to take a major decision like changing vendors, and even if they did, LTI would not be able to bag big outlays.

Naik's presentations to the C-suite were suffused with passion—he offered, debated, cajoled, coaxed, leveraged the L&T brand name and initiated a new and powerful system of 'barter'. The parent L&T would give firm 'A' an order for equipment or services for the engineering sector, and in return, 'A' would need to give an order for the software business. Under the compelling power of his persuasion, the companies began to open their purse strings, and the big orders started to come. The initial 'barter' was just the opening of the door, and subsequent business came in on the strength of service and quality.

Naik is also adept at cross-selling. Dileep Shevde revealed Naik's modus operandi to promote the IT business in the Middle East.

'He carries eight to ten folders for every business meeting, including one on L&T's IT capabilities, even if the stated objective of the meeting is something else. That's how he prepared for a meeting with the chairman of the Kuwait National Petroleum Corporation. Minutes into the meeting, Naik saheb sensed that L&T was not going to bag any turnkey contract in the hydrocarbon sector. So

## IT—A Vision Vindicated

he changed tack and started talking about the IT business,' Shevde recalled. "'Let me tell you frankly," Naik told the KNPC chairman, "your IT systems, such as they are, seem to be outdated. Let me send my IT team and help you modernize."'

Thus, what L&T lost in hydrocarbon, it gained in IT. This became standard operating procedure—the company's strengths and contacts in engineering and construction would be leveraged to build its IT business. Many of the big wins for LTI came from companies like Chevron. This is part of Naik's secret sauce which helped propel the company's IT thrust.

Naik also carved out three related businesses from the parent company and formed a stand-alone company, now known as L&T Technology Services. This company stands at the precise intersection of technology and engineering and empowers enterprises to ride the wave of digitalization and IoTization. The combined expertise of this cluster of companies enables L&T to contribute significantly to the PM's Digital India programme and build Smart Cities for the future.

Today, IT is everywhere. We can't do without it and we have come to accept that it is an inescapable part of our lives. Naik saw this decades ago and was relentless in pursuing the IT dream for L&T. The services business, which IT is part of, contributes around 30 per cent of the total company's revenue. Larsen & Toubro has also come to be seen as an IT company, in addition to being recognized as a leading engineering company and a nation-builder.

### Overcoming setbacks to success

Everything cannot be smooth sailing all the time, and for L&T in the IT sector, there were a few setbacks too. The most prominent example was the Satyam acquisition, which did not pan out as expected.

Satyam Computer was a clear case of corporate fraud perpetrated by its founder-chairman. When panic-stricken investors began jettisoning shares in the scandal-hit company, LTI was among those attempting to acquire it in a government-initiated auction. The attempt, however, misfired, and Naik later said, 'It is nothing but bad luck that L&T's plans did not go through,' despite being among the first to start accumulating Satyam's shares. 'The real story is that we were too early to get into Satyam,' he added.

It certainly was a setback, but it did not deter Naik in his ambition to make the company a major IT player. A few years later, LTI was listed, along with L&T Technology Services. The initial prices were not something to cheer about. But slowly, everything began to change. And then came the acquisition of Mindtree.

The Mindtree acquisition is a watershed moment in the history of L&T. It tells you a lot about the character of the company and the people who drove the deal—you need to push hard in pursuit of your dream because things are not going to fall into place all by themselves. You need to push past irritants and distractions.

Naik was given to rallying the troops with continuous encouragement. Months after the acquisition, he pepped up shareholders with the following letter:

Dear Shareholders,
The past year was a watershed year, as we successfully created an entity that accesses the benefits of scale, and

expands the array of offerings. By leveraging cross-industry expertise, we will also deliver greater value to all stakeholders.

This organization is integral to the technology-led strategic vision of the parent group, and will play a crucial role in the expansion and diversification of its services portfolio. Our client roster covers over 700 leading global enterprises from virtually every key industry vertical. Collaborating with them and building solutions for them are our team of over 84,000 highly talented professionals spread in thirty-five countries across five continents.

Together, we will continue to build win-win collaborations with our stakeholders, and hopefully, create a much larger force for new possibilities.

## The digital dawn

Today, LTIMindtree has a strong global presence across North America, Europe and the rest of the world, with an annual revenue over USD 4 billion.

New IT-related subsidiaries have sprouted, straddling what is now termed as the 'phygital' spectrum. Among them are L&T Smart World which seeks to transform cities into a smarter avataar of themselves—'smart cities' and L&T EduTech—a bridge between industry and academia to enhance the employability of those who graduate from colleges and institutes.

Then, there is L&T-SuFin, an integrated platform for buying and selling industrial products and services, with an aim to transform the B2B marketplace. Enabling businesses, especially MSMEs, to digitally and cost-effectively source their industrial suppliers from anywhere in India, L&T-SuFin is not just a digital marketplace; it offers assistance in financing and logistics support.

Naik is not as intimately connected with these new IT offshoots as he was with the old LTI, but he is always on hand to applaud, encourage and add to the josh (enthusiasm) quotient of the team.

At the inauguration ceremony of L&T EduTech in 2021, Naik said:

> I am very happy to inaugurate our company's newest public-facing platform ... I am sure this venture will open up new opportunity horizons for L&T, and will also help the youth of the country meet their aspirational goals. The central mission of L&T EduTech has always been close to my heart—provide teaching and training to the youth. I believe training is the key to transformation.
>
> L&T EduTech will bridge the gap that currently exists between what students learn in academic institutions and what is expected of them in a professional environment. Empowering our students with an industry-led practical and application-oriented engineering curriculum will be a boon for all—students, industry and society. Most of all, the youth will have the assurance that they are learning from a company which is known and respected as a knowledge powerhouse.

## IT—A Vision Vindicated

He ended with a nationalistic flourish, typical of Naik. He told the audience that to contribute actively to the India growth story during this period of accelerating changes, it was necessary not just to keep learning new things but also to find better ways to transmit learning. The new entity was another brick in the edifice of new India.

# 7
# Building Relationships That Last

*'My relationships are never transactional. My friends are my friends for their own sake, not for what they can do for me.'*

'Naik's networking ability is phenomenal,' says L&T's chairman and managing director, S.N. Subrahmanyan. 'He has met everyone on earth, and everyone on earth has met him.'

Even if you allow for a bit of hyperbole, it is a fairly accurate description of Naik's expansive bank of contacts. We believe his proliferating network comes from two basic character traits: he is interested in people and is insatiably curious. With a smile, Naik begins with standard questions like 'Who are you?' and 'What do you do?', but then he wants to know everything else about you—

what your family is like, where you went to school and college, what your goals and interests are.

His questioning sometimes crosses conventional limits and gets personal, but nobody really minds. After all, an octogenarian of such rare stature is allowed a few liberties. Most people also acknowledge that Naik's curiosity is not idle; the information he gleans will go towards painting character portraits of people in his mind. Also, his retentive memory ensures that he doesn't forget details. This also means that you need to be careful of what you say—you may have told him that your daughter is pursuing classical dance, but when you meet him months later, he might ask you when the arangetram is, so you better have an answer.

In 2003, when Naik was appointed chairman of L&T, it was the first time an employee had been elevated to that post—all the earlier executive chairmen had been connected to the founder-directors of L&T Private Limited. Naik's appointment was an acknowledgement of the pivotal role that people played in the organization, and L&T's in-house magazine hailed him as 'the people's chairman'. The title fit him well, because he had once said: 'I am not a design person or a salesperson. I am a people's person.'

Naik interacts directly with people across the board, and we found this characteristic easy to trace back to his youth. Had Naik grown up in the tony enclaves of Mumbai and studied in Ivy League institutions, he would probably have ended up as a clubby, somewhat snooty sort, interacting exclusively with people of his own 'level'. But he grew up seeing his father and grandfather interacting with the children of the village without a thought about their caste or social status.

A young Anil Naik with his family. Behind him are his father Manibhai Naik, mother Maniba and sisters Pushpaben (left) and Urmilaben.

Naik persuaded his ageing parents to relocate to his home in Mumbai.

With Geetaben—all smiles, all the way!

His only role model—his father. Naik once said: 'My father lit a lamp. I am happy that I could help more and more people see the light.'

From left, top: son-in-law Mukul Shah, son Jignesh, daughter-in-law Rucha, daughter Pratiksha; granddaughter Sharini, Naik, Geetaben and granddaughter Riya.

Three chairmen of L&T from different eras share a stage in a rare picture taken from L&T's archives: (L to R) A.M. Naik, Henning Holck-Larsen and N.M. Desai.

At the turbine shop in Hazira, set up as part of Naik's thrust into power equipment manufacture.

At the shipbuilding and repair facility in Kattupalli, on India's east coast near Chennai. The facility also incorporates a modular fabrication yard.

With Narendra Modi as chief minister of Gujarat.

A courtesy call on Manmohan Singh after he had given up office of the prime minister.

With L&T's first Indian chairman, N.M. Desai, who led the transition in the 1970s to management drawn from within the country.

With his team of executive directors soon after taking over as CEO.

L&T has built metro systems in major cities in India and abroad. Picture shows a metro system in Mauritius.

The A.M. Naik Tower stands just a few hundred metres from the gate to the Powai complex that a young Naik had entered decades ago with an application in his hand.

The Coastal Road in Mumbai reflects the growing pace and sophistication of urban infrastructure.

The 182-metre Statue of Unity—the world's tallest—inaugurated by the prime minister in 2018.

Atal Setu—the Mumbai Trans Harbour Link—is India's longest sea bridge.

Ram Mandir in Ayodhya, another of the many iconic structures built by L&T.

The Coastal Road tunnel built in Mumbai by L&T has been widely admired.

L&T has been associated with India's space missions almost since inception.

L&T participated in the ongoing global experiment in France to generate nuclear energy using fusion technology by building the largest high-vacuum pressure vessel ever built in human history.

On 19 January 2019, the PM took a ride in an L&T-built howitzer at Hazira. Earlier, he had inaugurated L&T's Armoured Systems Complex.

L&T played a major role in building the INS *Arihant*, India's first nuclear-powered submarine. (Picture for representational purpose only.)

L&T's facility at Talegaon, Maharashtra, dedicated to defence production, reflects L&T's commitment to serve strategic national needs.

One of the several coal gasifiers built by L&T for export to major markets, including China.

Chrome-Molybdenum-Vanadium reactors are among the most complex in industry. Picture shows reactors bound from Hazira to Kuwait.

L&T set another record in the heavy engineering space by building the world's heaviest LC MAX reactors.

End Shields for nuclear reactors. L&T has built almost all of India's indigenous nuclear reactors.

Giant oil and gas platforms built by L&T at its modular fabrication yard in Hazira near Surat.

A fertilizer plant—one of several built by L&T across India.

The world's largest pet coke gasification complex and ethylene cracker at Jamnagar.

A 2×660 MW power plant in Uttar Pradesh. L&T has also initiated a thrust into green energy by commissioning its first indigenously manufactured electrolyser.

A high-precision manufacturing facility for turbines.

L&T has built several water treatment plants in India and is recognized as the leader in developing water infrastructure in the country.

Receiving the Padma Vibhushan from President Ram Nath Kovind on 16 March 2019.

Receiving the Padma Bhushan from President Pratibha Patil on 31 March 2009.

In 2009, Naik was honoured with Gujarat Garima—the highest state award—from then chief minister Narendra Modi.

Receiving the Lifetime Achievement Award at the ET Awards, at the hands of External Affairs Minister S. Jaishankar in March 2023. Naik has been honoured by almost every major media house in the country.

The Economic Times Business Leader Award, presented by then prime minister, Manmohan Singh, in 2008.

The prime minister flanked by Naik's family and other dignitaries at the inauguration of the Nirali Hospital complex in Navsari on 10 June 2022.

Union Home Minister Amit Shah inaugurates the A.M. Naik School in Powai, Mumbai.

The old primary school in the village of Endhal, rebuilt and restored by Naik.

The Urmi Science Centre, named after Naik's sister, draws students from schools across the district.

A 500-bed healthcare complex in Navsari incorporates a cancer hospital, a multi-speciality hospital and accommodation for doctors and nursing staff.

The A.M. Naik School at Powai has emerged as one of the most reputed schools in the area.

A healthcare facility in Powai is a boon for the community.

Located in Kharel, south Gujarat, the Anil Naik Technical Training Centre is one of the few offering vocational training to unemployed youths with no previous qualification.

Tailoring is among of the broad spectrum of trades taught at the Anil Naik Technical Training Centre, Kharel.

Youths are trained in repair and maintenance of tractors at the Anil Naik Technical Training Centre in Kharel in south Gujarat.

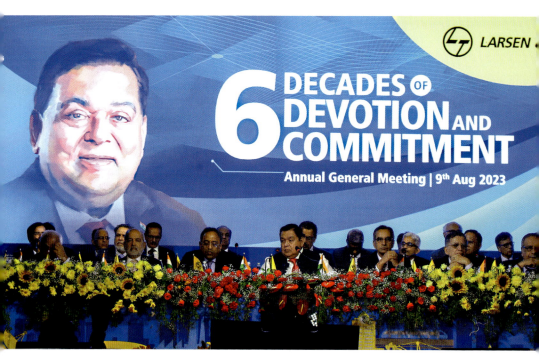

Naik's last AGM as chairman saw an outpouring of sentiment from shareholders for whom 'Naik saab' is a perennial hero.

In 2017, Naik handed over to S.N. Subrahmanyan a sword, symbolizing valiant defence of the company.

Smooth succession at the apex level paves the way for Naik becoming chairman emeritus of L&T.

# Building Relationships That Last

This characteristic of young Anil was noticed by many contemporaries in his early days at L&T. As mentioned before, he was not one of those who confined themselves to air-conditioned cabins; he would be out on the shop floor rubbing shoulders with workmen.

## Arre bhai, where are you

When he rose through the echelons and became the head honcho, Naik did not subscribe to the usual corporate communication protocol—CEO interacts exclusively with vice president; vice president talks to general manager; general manager talks to immediate supervisor. Instead, Naik just picked up the phone and talked to the person handling the job: 'Arre, bhai, where are you? Okay, come to my office right now.'

In the interdependent society we live in, it is being increasingly recognized that you can't do it all alone. Ideally, as the saying goes, you need to make friends before you need them. Naik's networking engine is ticking all the time, across geographies and all barriers of hierarchy. He networks with shop floor workmen, labour unions, his peers across industry, political leaders and celebrities. He reads people like one reads a newspaper; a few minutes is all it takes him to assess a person, suss out their characteristics and get to know their strengths and weaknesses. Often, it takes only a single meeting and a handshake for Naik to sow the seeds of a warm friendship.

Naik's people-skills have proved useful on many occasions: tricky problems that have left others at a loss have been resolved with just a phone call from Naik. But often, he networks when there is no problem to be solved and no gain in sight. He makes it a point, therefore, to call on those who are no longer at the top—retired bureaucrats, politicians who are no longer in power and former colleagues.

Subrahmanyan, colloquially known within the company by his initials 'SNS', who has been interacting very closely with Naik for the last few years, provides additional information—Naik leaves such an impression on people he meets that he is rarely forgotten.

'Even today, when I meet people, they ask me how AMN is. I ask them when they last saw Naik. They reply, "Twelve years ago,"' says SNS.

He adds that it is probably Naik's visible passion and his deep commitment that leave a lasting impression. Facts and figures about L&T turn fluorescent in Naik's narration, searing themselves on your consciousness.

'Even if he has had ten meetings in a day, and another meeting comes up, he will explain it the eleventh time with even more passion,' says Subhramyan.

Naik's concern for people fits in with the culture of the company. Long ago, when interviewed for a corporate film, co-founder Henning Holck-Larsen had said: 'Machinery must be there, buildings must be there, but without the people, it's all nothing.'

Years later, L&T also ran an advertising campaign with the tag line 'People—the Prime Movers'.

There is no denying that 'people' are a staple theme for many corporates; every company loves to talk about how much it cares for its employees. But in L&T's case, there is good reason to believe that advertising claims reflect reality. And Naik is its best endorsement.

# Building Relationships That Last

R.N. Mukhija, once head of L&T's electrical and automation business and subsequently, an advisor to the chairman, told us that Naik's leadership style transcends individual differences. Mukhija has a slow, measured way of speaking that invests every word with weight and significance. 'His operational style was very different from mine, but he never let that come in the way of our relationship', said Mukhija.

He has an invisible glue that makes employees bond with the company even though they have diverse views. Y.S. Trivedi provides a clue to the answer.

'How do you think people like us stick around for forty years?' he says. 'We know our value; we are opinionated; we are gold medallists—the best. We are forever getting offers and invitations to be poached. Why do we still stick around? I think the answer is Mr Naik. He creates relationships; we feel connected like a family. In a meeting, there is 100 per cent office decorum. Outside, we are family.'

## Prospecting for gold

When Naik visits a city, he prospects for gold. He seeks talent and opportunity. Nothing may happen at a dozen such dinner meetings but there is always the possibility that something will. We will call it 'assisted serendipity' when he chances upon a prospective customer, a collaborator or, in one memorable case, a future board member and director.

This happened at a convivial drinks-and-dinner party in the port city of Visakhapatnam, where L&T was engaged in building submarines for the Indian Navy. As usual, when Naik had an evening free, invitations were sent out to the who's who of the city. The invitees included a charming gentleman with a resonating voice—Shailendra Roy, then head of a prominent public sector unit.

Initially, Roy was not keen on attending the party, but his wife convinced him to. When he entered the room, Roy told us, he was a little surprised by the warmth of Naik's welcome.

'He seemed to be waiting for me,' said Roy. 'He gives everyone the impression that he is waiting only for you. There were many people in the hall, but he steered my wife and me to a secluded table. He started to interview me over a glass of wine. I wondered "Why the hell is he asking questions like an interview?" I told him it was more or less decided that I was joining Reliance, and added that I had already chosen the house they would give me.'

Then, Naik got down to brass tacks. 'Why don't you join L&T?' he asked.

Roy was taken aback. The salary he was being offered by the other prospective employer was very good, and it was unlikely that L&T would be able to match it. Naik then sweetened the offer by talking about employee stock options. Roy did not understand anything about shares, but his wife did, and was impressed.

Still undecided, Roy sought the counsel of D.V. Kapoor, a family friend. Kapoor happened to be on the board of both companies—Reliance and L&T—and was probably in the best position possible to advise Roy.

'Forget the salary. Join Naik. If you join Reliance, you will be just another face. If you work with Naik, you will grow,' he said

## Building Relationships That Last

without hesitation. Roy subsequently rose to the position of director on L&T's board.

The decided advantage Naik has is that it's somewhat easier to build a relationship with someone who is already a public figure. He's been covered so widely in both print and electronic media that most people he meets are already familiar with his story; they know they are meeting somebody special.

D.K. Sen, an L&T veteran and currently adviser to the chairman and managing director, talked to us about his experience with Naik in the Middle East. 'They would listen in rapt attention, as though he was their teacher and they his students. We were actually there prospecting for business but the roles were reversed. They wanted to hear his story—how he handles people, how he built L&T,' said Sen.

The top executives of companies would never treat Naik as a contractor; he was always the leader. So impressed were they that they would come down from their offices and see him off to his car.

'I have seen this in India, when a top executive of a Port Trust in South India finished a meeting with Naik and walked him to his car. It's happened with big dignitaries in the Gulf too. The respect they have for him is visible. You can see it happening in front of your eyes,' Sen added.

Multiple sources confirm such stories. One of them is K. Ramakrishnan, chief executive of L&T's Skill Development Mission. He is now in his sixties, but his zest for all of the company's endeavours belies his age. We asked him how Naik came across as a spokesperson for country and company to an international audience. Ramakrishnan replied that Naik could fascinate his audiences with the picture he would sketch of India's infrastructure prospects, and how L&T's capabilities fit in with the investment plans of major global players. He could marshal facts and figures, details about trends and their likely outcomes. 'By the end of it, they are ready to eat out of his hands,' he said.

## Small gestures, lasting impact

It is often not the grand gesture but the little touches that turn everyday relationships into lasting bonds. Naik will be there when you need a helping hand, offer assurance in anxious times or a word of comfort in difficulty. He may not be the most effusive in expressing his sentiments to those with whom he deals, but sometimes gestures say it all.

Two former colleagues, long since retired, were both diagnosed with a major illness. When Naik got to know, he rang them up that very evening and inquired about their health. 'Don't worry,' he reassured them, 'you are sure to recover.'

'The doctors are still doubtful,' said one of the colleagues, uncertain and anxious.

'You will recover, you certainly will,' asserted Naik, injecting into his voice the robustness of strong faith. 'And once you have recovered, we must all have dinner at my house.'

A different kind of anecdote is narrated by Noshir Kaka, co-lead of technology, media and telecommunications at McKinsey and founder of its global outsourcing and offshoring practice. Kaka, who is based out of McKinsey's Mumbai office, told us about one particular drive back from Hazira in the company of Naik and other directors. When their convoy approached Valsad, Naik had an urgent message for Kaka.

'You know that we are approaching your Iranshah Atash Behram,' he began.

This is a well-known Zoroastrian fire temple in Udvada, near Valsad, with a fascinating heritage, religious significance and beguiling architecture. It is a pilgrimage centre for the Parsi community. As a native of south Gujarat, Naik was aware about it too and lost no time in translating a good thought into a good deed.

'We can stop near the Atash Behram,' Naik offered to Kaka. 'You can go in and seek blessings—and pray for all of us too!'

Kaka says he's unlikely to ever forget the gesture. Of all the interactions he has had with Naik, the Udvada episode seems small, but of such strands is the tapestry of a relationship woven.

## How to win friends, Naik-style

Many people have told us that Naik is an instinctive builder of relationships. We doubt he has ever read *How to Win Friends and Influence People*, but many of Dale Carnegie's prescriptions come naturally to him.

Dileep Shevde, who has experience dealing with several VIPs in the Middle East, told us about Naik's phenomenal skill in nurturing relationships beyond the initial handshake.

'He sees himself as an equal to the highest and mightiest in the land. He can go to Joe Biden and will not be overawed or uncomfortable. He may not be dressed for the occasion or even be well-groomed, but it will not matter to him,' Shevde said.

He believes the source of Naik's confidence in dealing with people lies in his heart and his mind. 'Naik knows his stuff, and he is gutsy. That's a formidable combo. You can't wrong-foot him,' Shevde added.

Naik leaves an impression that is not easily erased, and for some, that is a cause for regret. 'He came into my life too late. I could work with him only for eleven years,' rued Shevde.

**Postscript:** We have used the word 'networking' to describe Naik's ability to form a bond with the people he meets. But perhaps, it has been the wrong term all along. 'Networking' has connotations of forming a relationship with the objective of gaining something in return. Like every business leader, Naik does that—he often networks with an eye on the long-range goal of advancing L&T's interests. But often, there is nothing to be gained and no discernible motive. For example, we are told by L&T's office in New Delhi that he called upon former PM Manmohan Singh long after he was out of power. There is no agenda in mind, Naik sometimes calls on people just for old times' sake. As he put in himself: 'My relationships are not transactional. My friends are my friends for their own sake—not for what they can do for me.'

# 8

# Building Tomorrow's People

*'I like building leaders. I have been doing it for fifty-five years and counting.'*

WHEN YOU HAIL FROM A MASTER KUTUMB (FAMILY OF TEACHERS), you don't need a classroom, blackboard or chalk to teach. It is part of your DNA, and all you need to do is keep the flame burning. Naik is continuously on overdrive—imparting knowledge, honing skills, building capability. In the course of our extended interaction with Naik, we have met him several times, and almost every time we came back having learnt something. This has happened with others too.

Former director on the L&T board J.P. Nayak explained it best. Though they are near-namesakes, Naik and Nayak are a study in contrast—while the former dominates any room he is in, the latter keeps to himself and could be thought of as being almost reclusive. Nayak tends to shut his eyes when in thought, almost giving the impression that he is not interested in the conversation around him. But when he does speak, his words are rich in observation and insight.

Nayak's speech in Mumbai at the flag handover ceremony on 30 September 2023 is remembered by every member of the audience for its razor-sharp depiction of Naik's personality traits. 'Mr Naik sees more in you than you do in yourself. The reason he may get upset is because you are not living up to the potential he believes you possess,' he said.

We have heard the same thing from at least two others—Dileep Shevde and consultant James Abraham. The implications are clear: you owe it to yourself to clear the bar that Naik has set.

Capability building is not something to be done only when Naik gets into mentor mode. As Nayak said, 'Mr Naik is a lifelong teacher.' Remember those apprentices on the Powai shop floor who swore by their works-in-charge nearly six decades ago? Since then, Naik's 'students' have covered a wide spectrum, ranging from staff to senior executives. Now, the lessons continue with the mentorship of business leaders being groomed to take over companies.

There are many among the youth eager to learn from the experience of an extraordinary Indian business leader who can narrate in simple terms what they would not be taught in the best business schools. Constraints of time and the inconvenience of travel prevent him from accepting many invitations to campuses, but one invitation he could not decline was from IIM Tiruchirappalli on its convocation day, and that was because it came from close friend and former colleague on the L&T board M. Damodaran, who would not take no for an answer.

When Naik asked what he was expected to tell the students, Damodaran, who is also a former government official and an ex-chief of the financial market regulator Securities and Exchange Board of India (SEBI), and knows the ways of the corporate world inside out, was clear: 'Just tell us the story of your life. I do not want a speech that will be written for you by your executive assistant.'

Obligingly, Naik went without any notes and began narrating his story, starting from a little village in Gujarat to reaching the top bracket of industry. The large audience of young men and women drawn from the finest schools and colleges listened in rapt attention.

Damodaran told us later: 'It was arguably the best convocation address I have ever heard. It came straight from the heart, no mental filter. He told it like it was.'

Naik got a standing ovation that lasted so long, it almost upset the tight schedule drawn up by the organizers. 'We had to tell the boys and girls to stop,' said Damodaran.

With such high praise, we simply had to hear this address. And since Naik's office had no record, we asked the institute for transcripts or a recording. Here are a few excerpts.

> I got my first lessons in leadership early in my days in charge of the heavy workshops. In my large workforce, there were some who were conscientious and some laggards—especially in the night shifts. I was determined that targets would be met and the pace would never slacken. I earned the reputation of being the 'Night Rider'; I would personally conduct surprise

checks in the third shift and make sure that everyone was on their toes. Naturally, this led to resentment, and sometimes to confrontation.

Friends, courage in the face of adversity is the number-one trait of leadership. I refused to back down—I have never backed down to anything in life! In the end the workers realized that 'Naik sahab' may be tough, but he was also genuinely human. I used to take personal interest in the welfare of the workers and their families. And many years later, when I was appointed chairman, the first in L&T who was not among the founder-directors, I was called 'the people's chairman'.

---

Growth in institutions, and, let me add, in individuals, needs a combination of two things that are sometimes seen as opposites—vision and attention to detail. One gives you a macro perspective; the other gives you micro detail. Some people say this combination works best in partnership companies because one partner has the big picture and the other gets into the nuts and bolts. But this is not necessarily true. You can, and must, blend both qualities, and if you manage to do that, you have an unbeatable combination.

I was one of the first in L&T to formulate a vision statement. It gave the organization direction, provided purpose and helped rally the team towards a shared goal.

## Building Tomorrow's People

Complementing vision should be rigorous planning. One of the first things I did as CEO was to draw up a 100-day plan, listing out what needed to be done and the time frame [for it]. I believe planning brings discipline into dreams. I used to look at every plan, every proposal, in depth of detail.

When you develop such a reputation, the word spreads—none of my subordinates will bring me a proposal unless it is 100 per cent watertight, because they know that errors and assumptions will show up under my scrutiny. I am sure they, in turn, apply the same standards to their subordinates down the line. And so, the entire system is toned up.

---

Now, at the helm of L&T, the media used to say that 'Mr Naik is heading one of India's finest companies'. That was good, but not good enough for me. I looked at global benchmarks—for myself as a professional, and for the organization. When you compare yourself with others in India, it is easy to pat yourself on the back. When you place yourself against the best in the world, you know exactly where you stand. I actively promoted internationalization of L&T's operations.

Doing business outside India is more than a change of market; it requires a change of mindset. You will not win unless you can deliver value on a sustained basis. To do this, you need excellence in every aspect of business—right from the first stage of negotiations, through manufacture, procurement and to final shipment.

And before I wind up, a few words of advice: As students passing out of this great institution, you will have many career aspirations to fulfil. While you pursue your legitimate ambitions in life, don't forget that you also have an obligation—I would even say a critical responsibility—to give something back to your own country and your own people.

Keep the fire in your belly burning. Remain positive, but don't be content. If you have met all your targets, it only means you need to aim higher!

Finally, your priorities in life must be clear. I am sure that all of you will rise high in life. Whatever you do, wherever you reach, never forget where you came from—your parents, your family, the institutions which shaped you and the country you belong to.

We read through the lines again. It is fair to say that it is a purple patch of prose on how to find purpose in life and how to make the most of your talent and skill. In short, life lessons couched in simple, easy-to-relate terms. We are sure that they helped the young students of the management institute look at the world and at themselves through an entirely new prism.

## Moulding the minds that mould tomorrow

Everyone accepts the crucial importance of the right kind of leadership for an organization or indeed for any form of collective

## Building Tomorrow's People

endeavour. Still, everyone also concedes that one can never build tomorrow all on one's own. Tomorrow is the outcome of teamwork. You need to find and coach the people who will help you in the task. And Naik was among the first people who identified human resources as a business function.

'HR is the driving force of the organization. It can take a company to stellar heights,' said Naik in an address to the company's human resource professionals, where he encouraged them to put in greater effort.

He also placed HR firmly within the context of the organization, and aligned it to business goals. This was a far cry from the HR that many old-timers knew. People had begun to think the HR people were there largely to check attendance, regulate leave and organize an annual, largely ritualistic, meeting with the departmental heads.

Under the 'new L&T' that Naik was building brick by brick, HR shed its old image. It came to occupy a dominant role—becoming as important as, if not more so than, some businesses—in the company. Veterans recall the new appraisal systems they were subjected to, the new processes that were put in place and the new leaders who would get the show on the road. Articulate HR professionals, adept at language and aggressive enough to make change happen, began pushing the envelope, and L&T employees soon woke up to the new realities. They also realized that they would have to begin the whole process of unlearning and relearning. The old order was changing, with a stronger incentive for performance.

In the old days, it used to be said that L&T was a kind old company where if you performed exceptionally well, you would be promoted in three years; if you did not perform very well and were just coasting along on the strength of seniority, you would be promoted a year later—not much difference. So, change would inevitably involve a degree of pain.

In a large company like L&T, it was inevitable that in some areas, complacency had set in, that the axe had to fall on some non-performers. But it was done as gently as possible.

Naik himself decided to communicate the message, explaining his rationale. 'Companies that are not internally competitive,' he told employees at several meetings, 'will very soon stop being externally competitive. And then, it will not be a few people we will have to let go of. All of us would need to go.'

Naik's ability to read character is uncanny. Academic credentials are certainly important, but that's something his assistants check. Naik just speaks to prospects and listens to their responses. An hour later, he has more or less decided who is in and who is out.

## A learning organization—24x7

This is a company that has been associated with the transmission of knowledge. In fact, the vision statement crafted soon after Naik took over states that L&T would be a 'learning organization'.

That learning is transmitted in unexpected ways. As J.D. Patil, adviser to the chairman, put it: 'Mr Naik is always in pursuit of excellence. Behind your back, he will praise you, but to your face, he will challenge you, goad you to make it bigger and better.'

This may initially be an unpleasant way of learning, but it works. Naik knows it well, and so should Patil—he was among the first batch of Naik's mentees. A decade later, Patil found himself on the board.

The LDA in Lonavala is another example of how tomorrows are built. Think of it as a base camp for mountaineers. You gear yourself up, are coached by experts and also rub shoulders with fellow mountaineers, sharing notes. This is a continuous process. There is always a greater peak to be summited, another 'high' ahead of you.

As mentioned in a previous chapter, the LDA was set up in 1997, a couple of years before Naik took over. It was initially called the Management Training Institute and kept a low profile, appearing diffident about its growth and direction. From being what would best be described as a backwater of L&T's learning initiatives, it assumed centre stage and soon began to see the arrival of professors from a host of prestigious universities around the world.

Naik helped the institute spread its wings—as with individuals, he saw in the LDA far greater potential than it saw in itself. For a start, the campus was expanded to over twice its size. The facilities were changed to accommodate state-of-the-art systems, including a telepresence centre that, we were told, enables a class to listen to a professor in Harvard, a consultant in London and domain experts at an offshore facility in the Gulf all at the same time. Yes, it is a kind of video conferencing made more expansive and offering enhanced reliability.

Gradually, the LDA's profile and personality underwent a transformation. The not-so-pretty duckling had become a swan! In tandem with the Seven-Step Leadership programme that Naik had conceptualized, the LDA began to advance towards its goal of creating a potent community of leaders and managers.

Change of a similar nature is evident in L&T's Institute of Project Management (IPM) in both Vadodara and Chennai. If the LDA deals with leadership development in a larger, holistic sense, at these institutes, the focus is on the nitty-gritty of projects. The crucial, make-or-break role that projects play in industry is being increasingly recognized. Projects built on time and within budget are a big boost for progress; mis-handled projects could, as they say, take the ship down with them. At the IPMs, the company's young engineers are taught the techniques for sustained success by the experts in the field.

As Naik said in his address to both chapters of the institute: 'We at L&T have been at the forefront of project management and have created an abundant wealth of knowledge in conceiving, planning and executing mega-scale projects.'

It is the kind of expertise that is the password to a more fulfilling tomorrow.

## Structured mentoring

Mentoring was not a new concept at L&T; it used to happen earlier too, but it was not a formal, structured affair. It was Naik who formalized it with a predetermined timeline set up by his office, rigorous appraisals and continuous follow-ups. As with many other things in life, a regimen and a structured approach make a big difference—they turn activity into an exercise.

Naik is by no means an easy teacher, but he is an effective one. He sets his standards almost unreachably high, and he is unsparing in his criticism. He will push his pupils, goad them on. It is a transformative process. At the end of it, sweating and cursing, his wards find that they have taken a giant leap. They are better professionals, with a wider perspective and a fuller understanding of the company's goals.

We asked S.N. Subrahmanyan what yardsticks Naik used to appraise talent. What did he really look for? He knew the answer, having been hand-picked by Naik and mentored by him for a decade. We reproduce his answer here almost verbatim.

'He looks for leadership, the ability to present oneself well, to articulate well and talk sense. I get the feeling that he homes in on people with a certain vision and direction. You will need to be certain of yourself and stand your ground, because he will see if he can push you easily,' said Subrahmanyan.

'He is inquisitive. He will ask you about the market, about competition, about people, and he will gauge your networking ability. You had better be good with numbers because he may suddenly shoot questions about market share and PAT. If someone gets it all right, Naik likes it and his feelings are visible. If someone fumbles, Naik frowns. I think that is perfectly fair. And when you go to meet him, you had better go well prepared. He is not expecting anything special from you. He is preparing you to face the outside world.'

Naik is focused on finding leaders. 'Once you find the leader, then find the position. Don't look for the position first. His logic is that once a leader has been found, you will be able to position him wherever you need', Subrahmanyan said.

# A.M. Naik

## Finding the right leader is half the battle won

Subrahmanyan has also adopted Naik's method of picking the leader before the business. 'I have also imbibed the same process. First, show me the leader. AMN has told me often—whatever you decide to do, make sure you get the best person as the leader. The right leader can make a bad thing go well, and a bad leader can make a good thing go bad. That is a clear lesson I have learnt,' he says.

One of the leaders he met very early in his career is K. Venkataramanan, who says: 'We learnt a lot in Naik's company. It does not have to be your regular mentoring session. If you are with him, you cannot help but learn.'

Another facet to Naik's ability to build leaders comes from Subramanian Sarma, the boss of L&T's energy business, who had previously held apex positions in the fiercely competitive arena of the Gulf. We were told by Sarma's junior staff of his ability to say a lot in a few words—where others needed an hour, Sarma could present his case in a few Power Point slides.

Such reports of Sarma's prowess, especially his outstanding expertise in the execution of hydrocarbon projects, reached Naik, who then began trying to get him to join L&T. It took a great deal of persuasion and protracted negotiations, but Naik is unstoppable in his quest for talent. Sarma was hand-picked to lead the hydrocarbon business after KV retired.

Sarma tells us of his earlier meetings with Naik having had no previous experience of dealing with him, he imagined that the meetings would be tough. But actually, they turned out to be surprisingly easy because Sarma was well-prepared, armed with all the facts relevant to the hydrocarbon industry and to the strategic location in the Gulf. 'You've got to know your facts,' Sarma told us, 'else you can't stand in front of him.' Fortunately, Sarma had these, plus the experience and necessary expertise, as well as the gumption to call a spade a spade.

A case in point was the proposal to boost L&T's presence in the Gulf. The project had been ambitiously christened 'L&T 2', and Naik had apparently devoted considerable time over it. Sarma stepped in with a different point of view—he wanted none of it; he wanted to dismantle all the preparations. Predictably, Sarma's staff recoiled in shock.

'How can you do that?' they asked, worry writ large across their faces. 'Mr Naik is not going to accept changes to something the whole team has discussed and brought to this stage. You are going to be thrown out of his office,' they warned.

Bracing himself for a firestorm, Sarma went to meet Naik, having marshalled all the necessary facts to buttress his argument. Naik asked several critical questions, all of which were skilfully fielded. Then, looking Sarma directly in the eye, Naik said: 'I agree with you. Go ahead.'

The point that Sarma made to us was that a real leader is not inflexible in his opinions. 'That's the quality of a great leader,' he said. 'Ego does not come into play. It's not my idea or your idea; it is simply what works best for the organization.'

Given his considerable experience in the upper echelons of industry, we asked Sarma if he has met another leader like Naik. He raised his head and gazed into the distance meditatively.

'I have met a few people who have a few of Naik's qualities. But nobody with all of them. He is like a million-dollar jackpot. All the numbers match.'

Naik invests a lot of time and energy in identifying the right people, persuading them (not everyone may be keen to uproot themselves from their surroundings) and grooming them to become the kind of leaders he is looking for. He is convinced that onboarding exceptional talent is well worth the effort.

We got confirmation of this from Shrikant Joshi, who himself had been selected by Naik to helm the fledgling L&T Realty. 'If you have talent, he wants you working for L&T. Whatever it takes, he will get you,' Joshi said.

**Personal guidance**

Formal mentoring by Naik takes place in waves. When each 'phase' of leaders matures, they will, in course of time, fill vacancies on the board, and the focus shifts to the next 'phase'.

'The first phase of mentoring is done on camera so the person who is being mentored gets a clipping; he can see where he did not respond correctly, where he could do better. He can constantly think things over and then, if he wants to, ask questions,' Naik said.

D.K. Sen was among the senior executives mentored by Naik. A large, affable person who looms over all those he deals with, Sen has a clear idea of what Naik's mentoring involves.

'It's all about developing a global outlook and thinking big. His scale of thought is huge and he will flit from business to business,' he said. This means that you could be handling Business X, but if Naik senses that your skills are better suited to Project Y, he will move you there without much notice.

However, Sen explains this is no bad thing. 'Trust him. If AMN has hand-picked you for a certain job, just do it. There is some plan that he has worked out for you.'

A.V. Parab has a perspective of Naik's mentoring that is distinctly his own. We gathered that it was like learning karate or any other martial art. The story goes that you first have to fight the teacher to become better than him. So the teacher pretends to be your opponent but he is actually there to teach you how to become a more skilful fighter.

With these words ringing in our ears, we looked at the young mentees keenly. We felt we could be looking at the CEOs of L&T 2040. We spoke to some of them for reactions to the mentoring process. Their responses ran through a common gamut of emotions—from initial nervousness to gradual appreciation to finally the full realization of the true greatness of the man before them.

Naik's mentorship programme encompasses many youngsters—part of an endeavour to bring down the median age of employees and make L&T a younger company.

The view that you can learn by just watching Naik in action is widely shared. Kruti Badjatia occupies a pivotal position in the company's structure, straddling the offices of both Naik and SNS. Everyone agrees that this diminutive but steely woman has a tough job on her hands—working with even one of the leaders on the top rung is hard enough; working successfully with both is a feat.

Badjatia is often asked questions by youngsters about the mentoring process. 'What do I need to do? How will I grow?' She has a simple answer: 'Just keep your eyes and ears open in Naik sir's room. You will grow.'

We asked one young mentee how he prepared himself for a session with the chairman. He replied: 'You don't know what he will ask. So I prepared for everything.'

We thought to ourselves, no matter how well prepared you are, you may still not be able to answer everything that Naik asks. But then it dawned on us—the preparation, the all-encompassing study, helps make you a better professional. And perhaps that is the point of the entire exercise.

Naik is, in a sense, a universal teacher; his 'class' is large, varied and growing. It's not just young mentees, executives or senior management, it's also members of the L&T board. Narayanan Kumar, independent director of L&T and chairman of the multinational conglomerate Sanmar Group, put it simply. 'Most independent directors join the board to learn. Boards, after all, are partnerships where there is a massive sharing of knowledge. Everyone learns at L&T board meetings.'

'Everyone' includes persons as sagacious as former cabinet secretary of India S. Rajgopal.

'I learnt a lot on how to deal with corporate problems, and I use that knowledge at other boards I am a part of,' Rajgopal said. 'This includes how to handle people, how to persevere with an idea and how to create a vision for the future. With promoter driven companies, they did not have the time to teach and did not have the time to learn. But with L&T, it is different. Naik loves to share.

So what he must have learnt from a hundred different people, I learnt it all from him.'

Former L&T finance head N. Sivaraman went a step further. 'Mr Naik is more than a teacher; he is a syllabus. Make sure that you read the syllabus thoroughly,' he advised.

We said suppose we learnt the whole syllabus by heart, would we be sure to pass?

Sivaraman smiled thinly. 'Not always,' he said. 'Mr Naik can also ask questions outside the syllabus, and you better be prepared for those too.'

## The best growth is self-growth

It is certainly a tough ask. But along with all those he's helping to groom and grow, Naik himself is also growing. He is, we dare say, also his own mentor. His former boss M.H. Pherwani had said that much of Naik's rise in his earlier years was due to 'self-growth'. That was six decades ago; it is still alive and kicking today. His energy flow is perennial. Those who have worked closely with Naik for many years are familiar with his burning zeal to do more, do better, do faster.

'He is evolving all the time, day after day,' said Chetana Patnaik, the ebullient chief human resource officer at LTIMindtree. 'Usually, when chairmen and heads of organizations achieve all that Mr Naik has done, they sit back content. But not Mr Naik. He is never content; he wants to act, contribute and get involved. It's an almost childlike spirit of "I want to do more".'

With that kind of mindset, it is not surprising that Naik seeks out people who share somewhat the same mindset. He finds many in the crop of young executives whom he mentors. Each of them is a proven high-performer, else they wouldn't even get there. It's no secret that the ones picked for mentoring by the chairman become the envy of the rest—although it is not publicly announced, word does get around.

We were curious about how the rest would react. It's merit-based, we were told. Not everyone is equal, and that is a fact that must be accepted. Since there's no favouritism involved, people tend to accept the results with good grace.

Further affirmation came from veteran Atik Desai, whom we have met in the chapter on Hazira. Desai asserted that 'only the best will make it through the "7 Steps" and the structured mentoring process'. When the HR department introduced the changes in promotion policies, they were not to everyone's liking. But that is the way the cookies crumbles. 'When you are the captain of a large ship,' said Desai, 'and you have to navigate it through a storm, you may have to take some unpopular decisions. Mr Naik did not succumb to the lure of popularity. He chose the path which was right for the company.' Eventually, everybody accepted that the changes were necessary to maintain the organization's keen competitive edge.

That's life—if rewards are evenly distributed to all and sundry, they would become just another routine disbursement. Exceptional individuals need to be treated exceptionally—this is the thinking that has shaped, and continues to mould, the new L&T

# Building Tomorrow's People

As we have remarked earlier, to insiders 'L' and 'T' stand for 'Learning' and 'Training', and few epitomize it as much as Naik. We believe his obsession with training stems from his version of 'divine dissatisfaction'. His keenness to continuously improve the state of things as they are is expressed in the facilities he has helped set up and in his relentless drive to sharpen skills. In 2018, when the Government of India made Naik chairman of the National Skill Development Corporation (NSDC), the appointment was accompanied by something akin to a citation. The skill development and entrepreneurship minister at the time, Dharmendra Pradhan, said: 'Shri Naik epitomizes the core values of a successful leader—strength, innovation, ingenuity, knowledge and foresight. [These are] values that are imperative to the success of any development initiative in today's economy. We are confident that the NSDC under his leadership should also be a think tank providing direction and necessary guidance for creating a demand-based skilling ecosystem in the country.'

Naik's appointment as NSDC chairman underscores the importance attached to skill training at the highest level. Prime Minister Modi has been stressing the psychological and social impact of skilling. 'Skilling brings a sense of self-confidence to the poor. Matching job creation with industry demand is the key to ending unemployment,' the PM said.

The government has drawn up ambitious plans to make India 'the biggest supplier of workforce to the world', and Naik is among those helping to turn this vision into reality.

## Training of trainers

Skill training of a very different kind is being imparted at another centre with which Naik is associated. The L&T Skill Trainers Academy stands at the opposite end of the training spectrum from conventional training centres. While the latter trains freshers or youngsters seeking growth, the former targets seasoned veterans. In other words, it trains the trainers.

Naik chose this model because its advantages are obvious—it is more resource efficient. When you train trainers, they disseminate knowledge and skills to hundreds of others, setting off a chain reaction that will soon impact a whole community.

As training locations go, the Skill Trainer Academy will rank among the more picturesque—it is on Madh Island, along the banks of a creek in a suburb of Mumbai. If you want to get there by road, you will need more than a couple of hours, so we did what most people at the academy do and simply hopped onto one of the many boats that ferry people across the creek.

A huge L&T monogram greeted us as we entered a campus that was as neat and well-manicured as all the company's establishments are. We learnt that before it became a training centre, it was a manufacturing facility for switchgear (one of the businesses divested by L&T and sold to European giant Schneider). In an even earlier avatar, it was a factory for drilling equipment—one of L&T's oldest businesses, long since discontinued.

Well, that was the past; the Skill Trainers Academy has set its course firmly towards the future. It was set up at the behest of the Union Ministry of Skill Development and Entrepreneurship and the National Skill Development Corporation. The company offered its facilities, put together an expert faculty and greenlit the future.

The academy's well-equipped classrooms are designed for interactive, experiential learning. It has state-of the-art laboratories and equipment to test domain skills. Since the programme is a residential one, there is also a well-appointed hostel with all amenities necessary for a comfortable stay.

In January 2023, the then governor of Maharashtra, Bhagat Singh Koshyari, visited the academy for 'Kaushal Utsav', marking the graduation of the first batch of 1,000 trainees.

In his address at this function, Naik said: 'Technology is constantly changing, and the techniques of imparting training today have evolved considerably. We have followed the policy of continuously incorporating modern processes and systems to make sure that our trainees derive the benefits of the latest developments in the field.'

He then talked about something he has been a long and tireless campaigner for changing public perceptions of blue-collar work.

'In addition to imparting skills, I strongly believe that we should also work towards bringing about a change in the mindset of large sections of our population. India has had a long tradition of valuing and respecting skill. As we all know, Vishvakarma [the Hindu deity of craftsmen] occupies a high position in our consciousness. But somewhere along the way, value systems have got distorted. We now place the blue-collar worker lower down the scale compared to his white-collar colleagues. This needs to change,' Naik said.

'India cannot claim its rightful place in society if people continue to believe that a desk job is better than a factory job. We look upon every trainee who comes out of this centre as a brand ambassador for skill training; they are also equipped with soft skills to give the world the message that skilled workers are vital assets to society, and can hold their own vis-a-vis their white-collar counterparts. India is fortunate that skilling is receiving attention at the highest level of India's political leadership. Prime Minister Narendra Modi's Skill India Mission has the potential to create a robust skill ecosystem. We at the L&T Skill Trainers Academy are proud to be doing our bit to turn our Prime Minister's dream into reality, and make India the skill capital of the world.'

The company's objectives in training align with the PM's goals. At the formal inauguration of over 500 regional training centres christened Pramod Mahajan Grameen Kaushalya Vikas Kendras in Maharashtra, Modi said India was preparing skilled professionals for the world, not just India.

Under Naik, and now Subrahmanyan, L&T too is doing its bit. It is winning national recognition for its efforts. In November 2023, a 'Skill Training Hub' set up by L&T in Mayurbhanj, Odisha, was inaugurated by the President of India Smt. Draupadi Murmu.

**Postscript:** Given his proven abilities and accomplishments, Naik was obviously a favourite target for headhunters across industry and geographies. They would lay out an offer—a plush office overseas, a bigger car, lip-smacking perks and vertigo-inducing emoluments. Naik said no to all of them. In fact, he had one stock answer: 'In this life, L&T.'

But there was one occasion we must record for posterity. One morning, a year after he was appointed CEO, Naik's phone buzzed. A Singapore-based headhunter was on the line. He began with the usual spiel—bigger responsibilities, amazing prospects, the works. Naik waited till he had finished his pitch before making a counter-offer: 'Look, there are a dozen senior executives I want to onboard, and I am looking for a talent-search professional. How about you come over to Mumbai?'

# 9

# What Sets Naik Apart

*'My mantra is simple. Passion, devotion, conviction, commitment.'*

A.M. NAIK HAS SEEMINGLY DONE IT ALL. HE DREAMED BIG, AND IS among the fortunate few who have been able to translate into reality much of what he dreamed.

As an industrialist, he orchestrated a transformation process that charted a bold new course for one of India's most admired companies, and enabled it to touch heights never attained before. The mantelpiece in his offices in both Powai and Andheri are filled with gleaming metal, tassels and congratulatory bric-a-brac. He has received almost all the awards one could wish for, including high national honours.

As a philanthropist, his outcome-oriented approach is making a tangible difference to the lives of thousands.

# A.M. Naik

So why can't we have more like him? How wonderful it would be if, as Dr Prathap C. Reddy of Apollo Hospitals once said, we had 100 A.M. Naiks?

We tried to separate the accomplishments from the achiever to decode his multi-dimensionality and find the answer to what makes Naik the man who built tomorrow.

## Macro and Micro

Some people believe that dreaming and doing are mutually exclusive. You can either be good at viewing everything from 40,000 feet, or you can bend over and study life through a microscope. Naik breaks the mould—he looks at the big picture and sees the brushstrokes too. This has been widely acknowledged by his peers.

For Naik, plans are pointless unless they are backed by demonstrable means to achieve them. In November 2017, at the launch of his biography *The Nationalist*, Reliance Industries chairman Mukesh Ambani underscored the point by saying: 'Vision without implementation is illusion.' Naik is too grounded, too level-headed, to remain under an illusion for any length of time.

He compels himself, and his team, to ensure that his vision goes through the grind—the shaping, bending and honing essential for it to emerge as reality.

How micro can you get? Naik will go down to the last decimal. No statistic and no long-term implication of a current transaction escapes his attention. He can recollect from memory the financial details of almost all the businesses within the company. He is not a visionary who will let others get into the granular details—he doesn't leave much number-crunching to others because he is a master at it.

## What Sets Naik Apart

Confirmation comes from an authoritative source—Subodh Bhargava, industry chieftain and a former director on the L&T board. Bhargava told us how impressed he was at his very first meeting with Naik. At that time, Bhargava was an independent director with Wartsila, the global power solutions company for the marine and energy markets. They were exploring the prospects of supplying engines for L&T's shipbuilding business. 'Naik came personally prepared for the meeting,' says Bhargava. 'He had all the details. Although his entire senior team was also present, they didn't have to be brought into the discussion at all.'

Alongside the ability to straddle both the macro and the micro, leaders have the ability to switch their minds and attention from one subject to another. Naik shifts gears without so much as a blip in conversation. He can be handling one business matter intensely one minute and switch effortlessly to another business or to a totally unconnected issue. From hydrocarbon engineering to CSR, branding to finance, corporate strategy to construction machinery—and each of them receives 100 per cent of his attention.

### Speaking your mind

We live in a world of pleasant noises, right notes and political correctness. You are not expected to say what you feel or express your opinion. Euphemism is the lingua franca of the corporate world, and the higher you go up the ladder, the worse it gets.

Naik is an outlier, known to be blunt. Even when talking to the media, with its fearsome reputation for amplifying the slightest misstep, Naik does not hold back. This has become widely accepted, and the media even has a word for it: 'Naik-speak'. It has many advantages, like telling you exactly where you stand, and saves time and energy because he doesn't waste them trying to sugar-coat his responses. It's either a yes or a no, often with the emphasis one would textually represent in capital letters.

He told us that if there was something to be said, even if it was going to cause some immediate unpleasantness, he would go ahead and say it. 'Otherwise, I feel it's a burden on me.'

As Noshir Kaka from McKinsey put it in conversation with us, 'Mr Naik has no filter.'

## Doing things differently

'We are prisoners of our legacies,' said R. Shankar Raman, L&T's CFO, blessed with a unique gift: being quick with numbers and felicitous with words. 'We are used to doing things in a certain way and begin to believe that it is the only way to do it.'

Naik, he said, does not subscribe to past practice or precedents. According to Shankar Raman, Naik believes that if things have been done in a particular way for a long time, it's an excellent reason to change things around. So when new ways of thinking begin to gain ground, the shackles of yesterday are broken; you find you can do more, do it better and faster. That's how Naik was able to be outrageous in his targets and expectations.

When Naik gave you a deadline, you would say to yourself, 'This is ridiculous. How is this even possible?' But then, seven or eight times out of ten, the tasks get completed. 'Those outrageous targets compelled us to find innovative solutions,' said Shankar Raman, 'which were always there, but were, so to speak, hiding in plain sight.'

# What Sets Naik Apart

## Scale of ambition

This is a term we have borrowed from Noshir Kaka. As a leading global management consultant, Kaka has a ringside view of the head honchos of some of the top companies in the world. He is privy to their thought processes; he can anticipate how they will react to a given situation; he knows what makes them tick. But he is clearly impressed with many of the striking characteristics of Naik. One of them is the awesome scale of his ambition. To use cricketing parlance, where most batsmen would be content playing a defensive shot, Naik would step out of the crease and aim for a six!

Decades ago, when a Supreme Court resolution made it mandatory for refineries to upgrade their systems, it opened up a large canvas for Indian manufacturers. Naik aimed big, and L&T got on to executing clean fuel systems at eight refineries simultaneously, all over the country. Observers across the industry said it would be impossible for a single company to do it, but Naik believed that it could be done and then proceeded to rally his team to make the impossible possible. This scale of ambition is also the propulsion power behind L&T's speedy growth in recent years.

'Dream no small dreams,' Johann Wolfgang von Goethe had said, 'for they have no power to move the hearts of men.' Naik would wholeheartedly agree.

## Human concern

Naik is not an easy person to work under; you need to be quick, sharp and accurate in your responses—not once, not twice, but time after time. Consultant James Abraham told us that he is a man who does not suffer fools gladly. Leaders who are so obsessively goal-focussed are generally known to be almost robotic in interpersonal relations. The IT industry is rife with chieftains for whom performance is all that matters—people don't. But there is a different Naik, who only reveals himself when his people are in trouble. Most of those who work for him swear by his concern. One of them said that if, God forbid, you land up in hospital, Naik will be the one who visits you, talks to the attending doctor and makes sure that you don't fall short of anything. We also heard from R.B. Anand, a former EA about how Naik had helped during a personal crisis. 'Naik saab is like god to my family,' Anand said.

**A visionary in a hurry**

There appear to be very few greys in Naik's mental spectrum. Everything is either black or white. It is probably this perspective that aids decision-making. You will never leave Naik's room without a decision. There is no dithering; one way or another, decisions come thick and fast. He may not win all the time, but in his way of thinking, to not decide is to lose by default every time. We are talking of major decisions—involving thousands of crores or on which the future of businesses hinge. But once all the facts are in, Naik doesn't waste time making up his mind. As the former chairman and managing director N.M. Desai once told us: 'Naik doesn't let the grass grow under his feet.' Being decisive and making sure that your decisions lead swiftly to desired results can put a lot of pressure on those around you. But we noticed that those who work in Naik's office do not let the pressure cooker atmosphere throw them off their stride. His secretary, the bustling Mario Fernandes, is cheerful at all times and on the busiest of days. And almost nothing can ruffle the quiet serenity of Naik's EA, Mugdha Trivedi. Incidentally, we must record here that Mugdha's efficiency contributed to bringing together the diverse strands of this book.

## Learner's mindset

Having reached the heights that he has, most people would tend to think there is very little left for Naik to learn. But his mindset is the opposite. He was an avid learner when he was young; he remains a 24x7 learner in his eighties. 'Observation is the key to success. Different organizations love different characteristics and styles. I would observe why Dhirubhai Ambani is successful and someone else is not. I keep analysing in my mind. My work habits are similar to that of an entrepreneur. You must practise it till it becomes a way of life,' Naik says.

This practice has always been part of him. One of his first bosses, the astutely observant M.H. Pherwani, had noticed it decades ago. 'Naik did his job beyond what he was expected to do. He acquired familiarity with finance, marketing, PR… Naik developed all those qualities,' he recalled.

More details come from Chetana Patnaik, who worked closely with Naik (and also with Subrahmanyan) as he augmented L&T's talent treasure chest. 'He is someone who evolves day after day. He has a transformational mindset,' she told us.

Whenever Naik has a business meeting, we are told, he observes everything about the person he is shaking hands with. What are their strong points, how do they approach a situation, what are the methods employed? In effect, he is constantly asking himself, is there something—anything—I can learn? How can I improve myself? This is his daily work plan.

It's this attitude that helped him bring about constant transformations within himself—from a village boy to the leader of a global powerhouse, from being able to speak only halting English to holding audiences in thrall with his eloquence, from knowing next to nobody in the corridors of power in New Delhi to being able to exchange ideas with the top echelons of the government.

Naik's reliable right-hand man, KV, told us he absorbs a huge amount from listening to people. The hunger for knowledge is continuous—one of Naik's favourite words whenever a conversation pauses is *aur* (tell me more).

We are sure that after going through this book, Naik's reaction will be '*aur*' too!

## Equilibrium of opposites

In October 2023, the magazine *The Week* carried a cover story on Naik, describing him as a happy coalition of opposites. Among the many things that set Naik apart, the magazine pointed to the felicity with which he could straddle two different worlds.

'Most people feel compelled to swear either by modern technology or by the glories of our venerable tradition. Naik faces no such dilemma. He is a vociferous champion of technology. In fact, fellow industrialist Mukesh Ambani once said that you only need to talk to

## What Sets Naik Apart

Naik once about some new technologies entering the market and he would be intrigued. Before you knew it, he would be incorporating the very same technologies into L&T's factories. But simultaneously, this technology aficionado is also deeply respectful of tradition... Naik's philanthropy encompasses extending generous grants to set up a traditional Vedic school in Valsad, south Gujarat, where the medium of instruction is Sanskrit. The school's aim is to restore the glory of our ancient land and re-establish the relevance of the Vedas. Naik is all in favour. After all, it is possible in Naik's world view to extol the wonder that was ancient India while exploring the new frontiers opened up by AI,' the article read.

Former cabinet secretary Rajgopal captured these unique qualities in a nutshell: 'Naik teaches industry how to play the corporate game while remaining ethical.'

## Leader Horizon 3.0

Large companies in a dynamic professional environment need to stay not just abreast of the times but ahead of them. At the helm of L&T, Naik repeatedly demonstrated his ability to anticipate the future. He could decipher patterns well before they became trends and re-mould businesses accordingly.

Some management pundits have described him as 'Leader Horizon 3.0'. These leaders build not for the immediate-term but for tomorrow. Naik built Hazira even when Powai was doing well, in the face of internal doubt. So when the opportunity arose, the company was ready. He has built several such facilities for the future—Vadodara, Talegaon, Coimbatore and Kattupalli.

# A.M. Naik

There are a clutch of other business segments that highlight his prescience: EPC (engineer, procure, construct)—a step up the ladder from pure fabrication—defence, aerospace, nuclear power, IT, technology services and realty.

## Leadership by example

L&T veteran, the suave K.R. Palta told us: 'Naik enters every meeting like a lion. Age may have slowed him, but the roar is intact—unquestionably the leader.' Leading by example is one of the oldest rules in the book. Almost all the leaders we know of have, in different ways, led by personal example. Naik has his own way—a hybrid model where he can both direct someone or do it himself, a general who can fight in the trenches. He can set daunting targets for the team; he pushes people to the limit, but they know that 'the boss' has set tougher targets for himself. He told us he would never ask anyone to do something he himself would not be able to manage. He tells people to be punctual, and he is always there ahead of everyone. He also makes sure the lessons are well-learnt by penalizing the laggards—buses will leave, chartered flights will take off and the doors to meeting rooms will be shut in the face of the latecomer.

The lessons he teaches go beyond business and industry and extend to philanthropy. Naik urges people to expand their scope of responsibility beyond their immediate family to encompass the country and society. He repeatedly tells his people to be more generous in giving. 'What you do for yourself is limited; what you do for others lights up the world.'

# What Sets Naik Apart

## Building team leaders

Who is a leader? We were given a rough-and-ready definition of leadership by one of L&T's former HR heads: 'A leader is one who can make others do what he wants them to do. Once he stops being able to do that, he stops being a leader.' Debatable, perhaps, but it certainly tells us how crucial the role of a leader is.

As we have said before, Naik is on a 24x7 search for leaders. Whenever a proposal for a new project or a new investment is taken to Naik, his first question is always: 'Who is going to be the leader?' Only after studying the credentials and appraising the calibre of the one who is going to head the project will Naik say, 'Yes, I will invest in that leader.'

Larsen & Toubro is a company that has grown largely organically, where talent growth too is organic. In this kind of professional environment, to bring about a cultural transformation and allow inorganic talent to flourish was a huge task. Naik was up to the challenge—after all, leadership transformation has been his forte all along, from the early days in the workshops to the C-suite.

This has also helped him overcome a hurdle common to many companies—the pangs of succession planning. 'I have always believed that succession planning is vital for an organization's sustainability,' he said.

When Naik stepped aside and S.N. Subrahmanyan took over the reins, everything played out as per script. There were no sudden surprises and no dark horses making an unsettling entry. Naik said that he had seen 'a spark in the man (Subrahmanyan) a decade ago'. How that spark was kindled and how it grew into a blaze is dealt with in the last chapter. Characteristically, thinking ahead of time, he has engaged with over twenty-five top executives to ensure that L&T has a robust leadership pipeline as far as 2040. Thanks to Naik, the new L&T does not have the sword of Damocles hanging over its head.

## Value creation

In his early days at the helm, Naik threw himself into 'value creation' with such vigour that it has become second nature for almost everyone in L&T, a tool for the transformation of the organization, from the corporate to the operating level.

Value creation is not restricted to creating products and processes; it also extends on an everyday level to such matters as fully utilizing every minute of every day. Naik is a master of logistics and sets great store by them. The fact that he was able to hold fifty meetings in a fifteen-day period in the US and three other countries speaks of his meticulous minute-to-minute planning—and, of course, inexhaustible stamina.

## Introspection: The everyday audit

We all know that introspection is very good for personal growth, but most of us are too busy to find the time for it. Naik is busier than most of us, but he unfailingly finds time to introspect—sometimes twice a day. It is usually on the way to the office or on the way back—Mumbai's clogged roads ensure he has plenty of time to carry out his clinical self-audit. He rates himself on his performance: How did I fare in that negotiation? Could I have done better? Is course correction called for?

## What Sets Naik Apart

The questions are deep and the answers are honest; otherwise, there is no point in the exercise. Naik himself has said the daily audit is one of the keys to success.

If you are keen to follow in Naik's footsteps, you know where to begin!

**Challenges are a tonic**

Most people, when they encounter a threat, focus on ways to protect themselves from immediate danger. Naik goes many steps further. His solution to the problem at hand includes making systemic changes so that similar issues don't crop up in the future. One would think that's just common sense. But it takes a lot of staying power to persist with an issue that has been already resolved until a lasting solution is found. Examples abound across his career: the vexing issue of attrition in the IT space, overcoming differences between collaborators (Naik made sure that L&T retained majority holding in all the joint ventures signed under his regime), and the biggest of them all—turning the takeover threat into a near-permanent defensive asset.

As S. Gurumurthy put it: 'The security risk that the company faced was converted into a security ring.'

**Mental acuity**

We are not sure if an eidetic memory and phenomenal powers of concentration are acquired skills or an inborn gift—winnings at the genetic lottery. It's probably a bit of both, with one complementing the other. Naik has made the most of what he has. In college he would hardly touch his textbooks for the better part of the year. Just one swift read a week prior to the exams told him all that he needed to know to emerge among the toppers. Later in life, this level of mental acuity has been an undoubted asset to the organization—even if it has been the cause of much grief among the senior executives who reported to him with business performance and plans. 'If you are not 100 per cent about everything that you are presenting,' one executive confided, 'you are walking on thin ice. You will be caught out.'

We were told that at the end of a two day-long presentation, when concentration levels had tapered, Naik was alert enough to spot a discrepancy on slide 19. 'Stop!' he said, holding up his hand. 'That's not the claim your team made yesterday.'

**Working long, making minutes count**

We left this for the end because it is the good old-fashioned prescription of hard work. Naik's son-in-law, Dr Mukul Shah, told us: 'No matter how brilliant you are or how gifted, if you are not hard-working, success will elude you.'

This may not find many adherents now, because we seem to have entered a version of the American Gilded Age. 'Work-life balance' is the new catchphrase many young men and women profess to swear by. The company's HR managers fret over Naik's work schedule—they fear it will scare away potential candidates. And then an iconic software guru stirred up a hornet's nest when he suggested that India's youth was taking it easy and ought to be working seventy

## What Sets Naik Apart

hours a week. Well, for the record, Naik in his time used to clock fifteen hours a day!

But all this is neither here nor there, and we do not wish to get into a debate about its efficacy. For Naik, it is intensity and not duration that counts. When Naik throws himself into a challenge, it would take a brave man to stop him and suggest that he enjoy himself. He is, in fact, having the time of his life!

His schedule now is less hectic than it was in his prime, and he does take the occasional holiday. But he still works tirelessly, with razor-sharp concentration.

And then, when most others would quit in exhaustion, Naik continues to forge on. Yes, relaxation is vital, for otherwise it could affect the quality of output, and Naik does relax, but his method of relaxation is to work some more!

As Deepak Parekh, former chairman of HDFC, once said: 'Naik doesn't know what rest is!'

Naik told us of a seemingly simple way to make the medicine sweet. 'Make work your hobby,' he said, like a happiness guru pointing the way to lasting bliss. 'Then you can work fifteen hours and enjoy every minute.'

Make every minute count, says Naik. If you can get something done in a spare minute, well and good; if you can get two things done, even better. Here is what he used to do often when hot on the quest of IT business in the US: 'Delta Airlines used to fly non-stop to New York. I would reach JFK Airport at 7 or 7.30 in the morning. I would get out of the airport, have my coffee at Starbucks, which is just opposite the office of my client Citibank. At five minutes to nine, I would be in the bank, having arrived from another continent.'

# A.M. Naik

We asked him how he gets over jet lag. His response was brief. 'Jet lag? What jet lag?'

**Postscript:** Multitasking may be a trendy new term. But Naik has been an inveterate multitasker for years.

L&T veteran K. Ramakrishnan regaled us with a description of how a job interview is conducted in the course of an extended car ride: Naik asks the candidate to join him in his car and opens with a battery of questions. By the time they reach the first traffic signal, he has grasped the prospect's capabilities, where they fit in and whether they can become part of his larger vision. By the second signal, Naik has fixed the salary and other terms which could be offered. By the third signal, his mind is made up. When the candidate steps out of the car, L&T has either a new employee on its rolls or HR is tasked with beginning the talent search afresh.

# 10

# Family: Pillars of Support

*'I owe so much to my wife. If it were not for her, I would never have been able to achieve whatever I have done.'*

HAPPY FAMILIES MAKE HAPPY SOCIETIES. AND IF THE FAMILY IS THE nucleus of the society, it can be said that the lady of the house is the nucleus of the family. She is the anchor, bedrock and pivot on which so much rests. In Naik's case, it is Geeta Naik. She has sacrificed a lot, achieved a lot on her own, and what is probably even more praiseworthy, facilitated achievement.

You will hear a lot about her from her children, but perhaps it is A.M. Naik himself who put it best when he declared that if it were not for her, he would never have been able to achieve all the things the country hails him for.

For her part, and to her eternal credit, Geetaben rarely talks about what she has done. She was a very young bride at the time of her wedding. Many decades later, Naik would say that she had both 'grace and beauty'. Well, what did she herself have to say about her husband-to-be? Her reply tells us a lot about society and the mores of the time.

'Nowadays, girls have ideas about what kind of man they want. At that time, you cannot imagine—your parents would fix everything and you'd follow. It was not your choice.' After marriage, Geetaben continued her studies. After all, she was marrying into a master *kutumb* (family of teachers)! She wanted to make sure she completed her graduation and Bachelor of Education even while taking care of their baby girl Pratiksha.

Her parents had made a fortuitous choice. 'I had never imagined,' she said, 'that we would ever get to where we have reached today.'

Although her husband has reached the pinnacle of professional success, Geetaben has not let herself get carried away by the heady momentum of his accomplishments or the family's obvious change of stature. She still espouses sturdy, old-world, middle-class values. Clear-sighted, practical and untouched by the corroding influence of affluence, she recollects the past with wry amusement. After Naik got a promotion, they were allotted an apartment in Pali Hill. It is a tony address, with practically half of Hindi filmdom staying in the neighbourhood, including Naik's favourite, the immortal thespian Dilip Kumar. But the building and its immediate environs had suffered neglect, swarming with overgrown bushes and weeds. Geetaben found it a wilderness.

## Family: Pillars of Support

'People would say I am staying in a jungle. The roads were desolate and we did not have a car at our disposal,' she told us. A snake had apparently been spotted in the compound, and her son, Jignesh, did not help matters by coming home one day and telling her that his friends in school had said the house was haunted!

But Geetaben soldiered on, managing to provide a comfortable home for her two schoolgoing children, her husband's ageing parents and his overriding commitment to the job. The family took the inconveniences in their stride; the bushes were trimmed and the lawn weeded. As for the ghosts, they must have heard about Naik's reputation at the office and quietly slunk away!

That was childhood for the Naik siblings—not exactly one long whirl of bliss, but a contented one.

In an interview with the media years later, Geetaben said: 'Soon after I got married, I realized that I was my husband's second wife; L&T was the first!'

This interview has been extensively quoted across multiple media. While it tells us a lot about Naik's work style, it also tells us about Geetaben's sanguine acceptance of reality. She was very young then, but even so, she demonstrated a maturity quite beyond her years and an understanding that hard work was essential for a putative builder of tomorrow.

'He was not born with a silver spoon in his mouth,' she said. 'He came from humble beginnings and his amazing accomplishments are the result of his own efforts. We have only supported.'

Geetaben also told us about another trait of her husband—he never holds grudges.

'Challenges may come up at home or with the extended family from time to time, but they do not linger for long. He confronts problems head-on, even when criticism is aimed at him. He deals with the issue at hand and moves on. Often, you won't even notice or know if something has bothered him. With so many responsibilities, he simply doesn't have time for grudges. He finds resolutions and then lets it go,' she said. We considered how this is exactly what happiness gurus tell us in their discourses, and here is Naik doing it as a matter of course!

## Unstinting support from children

We asked Jignesh about the sacrifices the family had to make in granting his father the space, time and freedom to pursue his goals and ambitions. He had a different take and told us: 'Sacrifice is too lofty a word. Instead, I'd say we supported Papa; we were there for him and we adjusted. It came naturally to all of us. Looking back, I don't think it was too painful for any of us, because we knew what it was all for.'

Well over six feet tall and broad-shouldered, Jignesh's imposing presence is softened with his easy, somewhat boyish smile. Before we go any further, we must add that if this conversation had taken place a couple of years ago, the location would well have been Silicon Valley—that was where he had relocated to, like so many Indians of his age. The US was an almost irresistible magnet for young talent, and Jignesh went on to join one of the world's leading tech companies. And then, one day, Jignesh and his wife, Rucha, decided to come back to India. They returned to their parents,

## Family: Pillars of Support

to their homeland and to the tradition of community service that Jignesh's great-grandfather had started more than a century ago.

Although Jignesh had been out of India for twenty-nine years and Rucha for almost twenty, she said: 'We always had it in the back of our minds that at some point we would come back. Come closer to the family. They were there when we needed them. Now, we should be there when they potentially need us.' Simply put and carrying a key message for all children everywhere.

Jignesh lives up to his filial duties. Practically every fortnight now, he drives down to Navsari to oversee operations of his father's trusts.

Pratiksha, Naik's daughter, elder to Jignesh by a few years, is pursuing a career as a doctor in Louisville, USA, along with her husband, Mukul. We spoke to this couple and their two lively daughters over the phone, and all of them were eager to talk about A.M. Naik.

Pratiksha's earliest memories are of being taken to see Papa's office in Powai. 'I remember that he used to manage the shop floor,' she said. 'It was a large place with gleaming machinery and many people in uniform. We used to marvel at the equipment and the respect that he obviously commanded in his team. In a way, we became part of his world. Even when he worked on weekends, we knew it was very important work. What he did, the impact he created, everything was right in front of our eyes.'

Although Naik could not accompany them to their extra-curricular activities, he always kept himself abreast of his children's studies. They could count on him for support in every aspect of their lives. When they needed him, he was there.

In today's context, this may not have been the ideal work-life balance, but young Pratiksha and Jignesh, stewarded by their mother, were happy to accommodate. 'This was life.'

The only real vacation they had in those days was during Diwali, when Naik made sure that the whole family—grandparents, cousins et al.—came together in Endhal.

'Papa missed out on spending time with us when we were growing up,' said Pratiksha. 'But he made up for it when my kids were born by taking us on at least one vacation every year. Both my children loved it. Their faces really light up when we recall those times.'

Both children agree that when their father was at home, he was 'there' 100 per cent. They may not have sensed it then, but it was yet another example of their father's well-known ability to compartmentalize his thought processes. It made it possible for him to switch on, switch off and juggle his responsibilities with no overhang. While they wished for more time with him (which young child wouldn't?), the quality of attention that he provided during those moments compensated for his long periods of absence.

Despite being so deeply, almost inextricably engaged with the company, Naik is at heart very much a family man. Son-in-law Mukul put it graphically. 'He is the sun of the family. We all revolve around him and gravitate towards him. If there are twenty members of the family around him all the time, he is the happiest.'

Mukul is struck by the mental agility his father-in-law consistently demonstrates. 'I cannot multitask,' he confessed. 'I have X and Y chromosomes, but he is blessed with a thousand Xs—he can deal with matters related to his work, with the large conglomerate that he is helping to run. And without missing a beat, he can draw up

## Family: Pillars of Support

our holiday schedules—where to go, what to do, whom to visit ... everything.'

Families often face the residual after-effects of a crisis that emanates from the workspace. But Mukul told us that Naik managed to insulate the family with a fair degree of success.

'At times, we could, of course, sense that there was a problem,' Mukul said. 'But it is not as if he lost his cool or got short with us. On the whole, he handled it all with grace and finesse. My guess is that because he can multitask at so many levels, he can shut off one side of his brain and focus on the other, and then go back and forth.'

Well, it takes a doctor to dissect a personality and come up with this kind of analysis!

Mukul also gave us a peek into the private side of Naik—the side that has never made it into the media or documentary films made about him.

'My father-in-law invokes God's blessings every morning,' said Mukul. 'And the next thing he does is pray to his parents. Now that is not something you can teach people. When we see that, our kids also see it, and it's truly something we learn.'

On an impulse, we asked Mukul if there was a chink in Naik's armour, and he pointed to his stubbornness when it comes to looking after his own health. 'When we tell him not to do something, that's what he goes and does first. We tell him not to eat anything sweet, and he will promptly go and have a mango!'

If there is one characteristic that unites the family across generations, it is humility. Despite having the means to indulge in opulence, they choose a relatively modest lifestyle. Ostentatious extravagance is a no-no. They would rather make a name for themselves by contributing positively to their professions and extending a helping hand to others.

From their parents, Pratiksha and Jignesh have learnt a rare, difficult-to-sustain virtue—humility. 'My brother and I often hear people telling us they can't believe we are Mr Naik's daughter and son. "How grounded you both are!"' Pratiksha recalled.

Perhaps they acquired this trait from their father—he is as grounded today as he was when he walked into L&T's campus six decades ago. All this is despite the long, interminable list of honours that have come his way, including the Padma Vibhushan, Padma Bhushan, a clutch of doctorates and Lifetime Achievement Awards from virtually every media house, including, most recently, one from *The Economic Times*. The awards, trophies and medals are stacked high in L&T's Experience Centre in Powai, but their recipient never lets himself get carried away by the honours conferred on him.

## 'Mother is the hero'

Pratiksha and Jignesh think the world of their mother. Down-to-earth, level-headed and blessed with the ability to manage many things in parallel. No wonder that for both siblings their mother is 'the real hero'. Rucha joins them in whole-hearted admiration. In fact, she is always gushing about her mother-in-law, giving her credit for raising two amazing children.

## Family: Pillars of Support

'Like our father,' Pratiksha said, 'Mummy too is sharp, intelligent and capable of connecting with anyone. While she could have embarked on her own entrepreneurial journey, she dedicated her life to keeping the family safe, secure and thriving. My mother is behind the success of my father.' Naik would be the first to agree.

At every function to felicitate him for one professional milestone or another, Naik makes it a point that the spotlight is turned on his wife. Naik also recalls with gratitude that it was his wife who took care of his ageing parents, their two children and the hundred other things that crop up in a household.

In his last address as chairman to the shareholders in 2023, he said: 'All through this long journey, my family has been an immense source of support and encouragement. My wife has been my pillar of strength.'

### The 'daughter–father' equation

Jignesh got married to Rucha Nanavati in 1998, and she took next to no time to become part of her new family and look upon Naik as a father. 'Our equation is very much like daughter–father,' Rucha told us. 'I have argued with him about all kinds of things and made up just as quickly and lovingly.'

Naik reciprocates the sentiment. When Rucha first met his colleague S.N. Roy, he had said to Naik, 'Oh, so this is your daughter-in-law.' Naik interjected: 'My *daughter*.'

'I must confess, I knew I was being spoilt!' Rucha said to us.

Like her a daughter who is entitled to ask anything of her father, Rucha said at Naik's eighteenth birthday ceremony: 'While everyone is showering you with gifts today, I am asking something of you. I want you to take care of your health. We still need to learn a lot from you. We need your guidance on the way ahead.'

Rucha is more outgoing and vivacious, more of an extrovert, making a perfect foil to her husband. Along with the rest of the family, Rucha too is swept along in the momentum generated by Naik. 'He is always planning and executing. Even on holiday, when he is drawing up a schedule, he will factor in the time taken in the elevator and then to the parking lot. It's a never-ending cycle. Once, I told him I wanted to gift him a book: *The Art of Doing Nothing*. Of course, he was not interested,' said Rucha with a smile.

Hearing all this, you would imagine that Rucha is a laid-back, easy-going person. But in reality, she is pretty driven herself. She works for a leading Indian corporate and has notched up a string of successes that has propelled her to the top rungs of her profession. Tasked by Naik to oversee operations at his school and hospital in Powai, Rucha has integrated these responsibilities into her schedule with a precision that Naik would be proud of. She visits the A.M. Naik School and the Nirali Hospital periodically to ensure that everything is as per plan.

---

Priti Raut is Naik's niece, his sister's daughter. But she is much, much more.

She grew visibly emotional when she told us: 'He is like a father to me. I lost my father when I was just fourteen. Since then, Mama

## Family: Pillars of Support

has been everything to me. He made sure that I never miss my father.'

Priti is a trustee of the Kharel Education Society and has proven to be an asset in many of Naik's assignments. She began by streamlining the accounts and moving everything online rather dealing with cash. She also brought in all-round efficiency in operations and was able to save substantial money for the trust. The savings came in handy for maintenance and other expenses around the school.

These and other incidents augmented Naik's confidence in his niece.

'He knows that when a task is assigned to me, I will do it almost perfectly,' Priti said. 'He believes in me. And I will never let him down.'

As he has shown in every other sphere, Naik has the remarkable ability to inspire those who work around him and win their trust.

### 'If I had a do-over, I'd spend more time with family'

When asked what he'd do differently if he could go back in time and rebuild L&T, Naik acknowledges that in the 1960s, given the limited resources and lack of technology, there wouldn't have been much he could change. However, if he were starting over in 2023, given the technology, infrastructure, travel connectivity and other facilities, he would ensure to spend more time with his family. Nevertheless, he believes he could have done more for them, got himself more involved and been there during their unspoken moments of need.

As his responsibilities grew and vision expanded, his travel increased, and time at home grew scarcer. Occasionally, but not often, family functions did not have the head of the family present. But his family rose to the occasion every time this happened; and Geetaben was always there as the central pillar of the Naik household.

Naik's business instincts are so keen as ever, but he also relishes the role of an indulgent grandfather. 'If Nirali were alive today, she would have been nineteen years old. My grandfatherly instinct kicks in naturally when I see young girls of the age my granddaughter would have been,' Naik admitted.

'When I see a young woman, I automatically switch gears into father and grandfather mode, and help in every way I can, sometimes even unasked. I inquire about their marriage plans, their visions for the future … Rucha often tells me that I'm intruding into their personal lives. It's hard for me to explain that in talking to them, I'm envisioning a conversation I'd have with my granddaughter.'

---

## The doting grandfather

It is said that grandchildren are the greatest joy of their grandparents. Naik has watched his granddaughters—Pratiksha's daughters, Riya and Sharini—grow from tots teeming with mirth and mischief into lovely young ladies. As grandpas do, as if by instinct, he taught them what he knows of life, and that is an encyclopaedia in itself.

'Always be fearless', he would say, and it became a mantra for the family. Elder granddaughter Riya told us: 'No matter what the obstacles are, I tell myself not to be afraid. When I was younger, any time I felt low, Nana would put me on his lap and give me a priceless psychological boost. He would tell me that I am strong, beautiful and brave. Hearing him, I would inevitably be charged—yes, I can achieve anything I put my mind to.'

Younger granddaughter Sharini has learnt a lot from Naik too. 'We've learnt from our grandfather how to stand on our own. Looking at him and learning from him has given me the confidence to start on my entrepreneurial journey.'

For emphasis, she added: 'I will do it the A.M. Naik way!'

Every time Naik gets featured in the media, his grandkids whoop with joy. Sometimes, they also feel a twinge of apprehension—can we ever match those levels, they ask themselves. Well, Naik himself had once harboured the same doubts—would he be able to match his father's and grandfather's level of contribution to society? Well, history has shown us what exactly he has done. No doubt, the tradition will continue.

**TV talent show buff**

Life lessons aside, there are many other happy moments the family have shared with Naik. Having given up executive responsibilities in 2017, he finds more time to spend with his family than he could before. He throws himself zestfully into life around him. Jignesh provides numerous instances. As a student in college decades ago, the young Naik would confound his professors by attending the cinema theatres with greater regularity than the classroom. His fascination with films continues, and now he has more time to enjoy them.

'Papa loves watching talent shows, movies and wildlife documentaries,' Jignesh told us. 'He immerses himself in them completely. Once, he invited a talent show winner to our home and celebrated his success. Then, there was the time he saw someone win fifty lakh rupees on the popular quiz show *Kaun Banega Crorepati*. As it turned out, the winner was from Chikli, a village near my grandfather's hometown in Gujarat. Papa invited the young man over for tea and offered him tips on managing his newfound wealth.'

Sharini had something to add about how her grandad reacts to what is shown on television. 'When he watches a show, he doesn't just sit back and watch it passively; he gets into the act and he brings it to life,' she said animatedly.

'One time, while watching *Animal Planet*, he was so fascinated by the wildlife in Africa that he promptly booked a family holiday to experience it first-hand,' recalled Riya.

His granddaughters added that their grandad loves to sing and dance while watching Bollywood films. 'And the best part is he gets us both, and sometimes the whole family, to join in!'

So, while the whole world might know Naik as a doyen of industry, a hard-driving corporate honcho for whom work is 24x7, those who get to know him well, see there's another side—at the core of his being, there is an affectionate, caring family man.

## Family: Pillars of Support

**The darkest hour**

There is one chapter in the Naik family saga that will forever be bookmarked with grief. It is about Nirali, born on 3 February 2005 in Chicago to Jignesh and Rucha. She was A.M. Naik's third grandchild, after Pratiksha and Mukul's two daughters, Riya and Sharini.

Cuddly, with a quick, radiant smile that carried just the hint of impish mischief, Nirali took no time at all to become the darling of the family, the apple of everyone's eye. Photographs of those times show the doting grandfather giving Nirali a piece of her first birthday cake in a gaily decorated house. Friends and family members would say Nirali looked very much like Naik, especially her nose and chin. Everyone agreed that of all the grandchildren, Nirali took after him the most. Those family get-togethers were picture-perfect moments of bliss. Unfortunately, it was all too good to last.

When she was just sixteen months old, she contracted a seemingly innocuous fever that turned out to be the first indication of a rare form of blood cancer. The news sent shock waves through the family. Naik flew to the US, summoning all his resources and his vast network of contacts to help. Medical opinion held that it was possible that a bone marrow or cord blood transplant could help the child. The family pinned all their hopes on a transplant, and the quest began to find a matching donor. Many people and organizations volunteered to register as potential bone marrow donors. While a bone marrow match wasn't possible, they did find a cord blood match, and her transplant treatment began at Duke University Hospital in North Carolina.

## A.M. Naik

Through all the torturous twists and turns of advanced medical treatment, in her ward at Duke University Hospital, Nirali remained a cheerful child. But as fate would have it, complications arising from the treatment proved to be too much. When she passed away on 27th April 2007, Nirali was all of two years and two months old.

The family was devastated, each member asking themselves: 'Could things have been different? Could we have done more?' As Naik said: 'No one in our family has been able to fully recover from this tragedy. In my room, there are just two photos—one of my granddaughter and the other of my father sitting in a chair, with me standing beside him.'

When he narrated all this, we couldn't help noticing that his eyes had welled up. The depth of this emotional experience drove Naik further and deeper into a life of service to humanity.

Slowly, inexorably and inevitably, life has to go on. As Franz Kafka said: 'Everything that you love, you will eventually lose, but in the end, love will return in a different form.' Jignesh, Rucha and the rest of the bereaved family found their way back from the depths of pain and turned their grief into a step benefitting thousands of people, enabling them to gain access to advanced medical technology. In a sense, they were echoing Anil's father Manibhai Naik's cardinal principle: 'think of others'. Jignesh and Rucha became the newest torchbearers of the family tradition of service.

Three years later, the Nirali Memorial Medical Trust was ready to formally begin its mission of healing. It was a mission that would spread its arms expansively across south Gujarat and Mumbai, and provide advanced medical care to the needy. Truly, Nirali's radiant smile continues to light up lives.

## Family: Pillars of Support

Simultaneously came the Naik Charitable Trust, which built schools and a unique skill training centre. These are, of course, very different from hospitals and clinics, but A.M. Naik points to the common goal: 'Both my trusts are connected to life; one protects life, the other transforms it.'

We will be visiting each of the places of transformation in the next chapter, beginning with the flagship project that was inaugurated by the Prime Minister of India.

# 11

## Giving Back, the Naik Way

*'My father lit a lamp. I am happy to help more and more people see the light.'*

AROUND 9.30 ON A CRISP JUNE MORNING IN 2022, RESIDENTS OF Navsari, near Surat, heard the whirring of a helicopter poised to land. Top police officials belonging to the Gujarat police as well as the National Security Guard were on duty, keeping vigil around a patch of land adjacent to the usually busy National Highway 48. The elaborate, multi-tier arrangements made it clear the helicopter was carrying no ordinary visitor to this small, somnolent town steeped in history; it was Prime Minister Narendra Modi.

As a political figure, Modi rarely attends any private functions, even when it is the inauguration of an institution that would serve the public good. There are protocols to be followed, conventions to be respected. But here he was, at the Nirali Cancer and Multispecialty Hospitals, at the invitation of A.M. Naik.

Modi was greeted at the foyer by Naik and his immediate family. He then turned around to wave to the large crowd (of which we were a part), all of whom were eager to catch a glimpse of arguably one of the world's most charismatic leaders, whose popularity surges across large parts of the world. Courtesies done, Naik and son Jignesh escorted the PM around the sprawling 500-bed complex. This was no cursory visit, because Modi does almost nothing cursorily. Walking with his trademark briskness, he took a tour of the key facilities—the diagnostic centre, laboratories, operation theatres and neurosurgery centre.

Details were sought: How many surgeries had been conducted? What were the facilities offered at the hospital? How many radiotherapy sessions had been completed? What support services were offered? Where were the medical staff accommodated?

Consultants provided detailed answers, assuring him that the facilities were truly state-of-the-art and that accommodation for many nurses and paramedical staff had been provided within the A.M. Naik Healthcare Campus.

Later, at the formal function held under a shamiana erected within this campus, the PM inaugurated the hospital complex. He then went online to declare the Anil Naik Technical Training Centre (ANTTC) in Kharel a 'Centre of Excellence'. Modi publicly lauded Naik's social causes and his contribution towards augmenting the healthcare system of the state. In response, Naik told the audience that the activities of his trusts were in line with the national goals that the PM had set—Health for All and the Skill India Mission. Naik added that he was continuing a tradition of service that was begun nearly 100 years ago by his grandfather and carried forward by his father.

Naik's public-spiritedness, which Modi referred to, is widely acknowledged. In 2023, for the third year in a row, Naik was voted 'India's most generous professional manager', according to a survey published by the Hurun Report—the world's largest compiler of 'rich lists'. Significantly, it is not a list of those who have made the most money but those who have put in the most money towards public good.

## Healthcare: Fulfilling his father's dream

The Nirali Cancer and Multispecialty Hospitals are the latest in a long list of Naik's healthcare initiatives. It is a story of caring that, interestingly enough, had begun just twenty-five kilometres from this hospital—in the small village of Kharel in 1995. Naik's father, Manibhai, a retired school principal and devout Gandhian, had talked to his son about the general hospital in his native village of Kharel. 'It is a good hospital that helps many poor villagers, and right now it is short of funds. If you can help, help.'

It was only a suggestion, not even a request. But to Anil Naik, a suggestion from his father, no matter how mildly phrased, carried the imperative authority of a command. He immediately decided that he would help. But there was one problem—he didn't have the money. That didn't deter him, though; the money required could be found.

## A.M. Naik

Many decades later, and in a slightly different context, Naik would be quoted in an interview saying: 'You don't need a lot of money for philanthropy. What you need is a generous heart. *Dil chahiye.*'

Before the week was over, he had contacted the authorities at the Kharel General Hospital and sought details about their expansion plans. A sum of ₹4,00,000 he learnt, was needed to build a new wing. Naik checked his bank account and came to the conclusion that even if he withdrew all his savings, he would still fall far short of the target. In a similar situation, most people would have dropped the plan and explained their predicament. But Naik can't easily be stopped when he gets into mission mode.

He knew there was another source—the accumulated savings in his Provident Fund. He tapped into his PF account, and after withdrawing all that was permissible under the rules, he finally managed to put together the sum needed. He sighed with relief; it was a job well done.

But there was yet another surprise hurdle—his father's scruples. Gandhiji had said the end could never justify the means, and Manibhai Naik believed that even if you are doing good, you must do it the correct way. He had a niggling doubt—was everything in order? Did his son cross the line somewhere in his enthusiasm to help? If so, the fiercely principled old man would not touch a penny. So Naik quickly began collating all the documentary evidence he could lay his hands on—a copy of his application to L&T for withdrawal of his PF, his salary slip, which he had never previously looked at, and his bank details.

## Giving Back, the Naik Way

Manibhai perused each of the documents and, satisfied at last that every rupee had been fairly earned, he handed over the cheque to the hospital. This led to the setting up of a modern wing at the hospital, named, appropriately enough, after Naik's grandfather Nichchhabhai Naik. Respect and love for one's parents obviously runs deep in the family.

There was another happy consequence: it added a new dimension to the way father regarded son. Until then, whenever Manibhai's old friends would comment that Anil was faring well as a high-ranking executive at L&T, Manibhai would merely nod in agreement. But after work on the hospital began, his response was qualitatively different: 'Yes, I am proud of my son because he is thinking of other people. He is putting the welfare of others above his own!'

Those were sentiments that Naik cherished in the deepest recesses of his heart. It also encapsulated a lifelong lesson: think of other people. After all, thinking about oneself is an instinctive, probably essential, human attribute. But you become a greater human being and climb a rung of the evolutionary ladder when you include the well-being of others in your thoughts.

Many centuries ago, Gujarat's saint-poet Narsinh Mehta composed a song that grew to become Gandhiji's favourite hymn— '*Vaishnava jana to tene kahiye je peed parayi jaane rey*' (The one who understands the pain of others is a man of god). Thinking about the welfare of others went on to become a personal motto for Naik—a message that resonated through all his actions. It led him years later to set up his two trusts: the Naik Charitable Trust and the Nirali Memorial Medical Trust.

# A.M. Naik

## As good as the best in the world

The Nirali Cancer and Multispecialty Hospitals are part of the expansive Naik Healthcare Campus, which includes accommodation for doctors and paramedical staff.

What struck us immediately as we stepped through the gates of the cancer hospital in Navsari was its quiet aura of clinical efficiency. This did not seem like a small-town hospital. This hospital could be in any Indian metro, or even in Europe or the US.

When we mentioned this to Jignesh Naik, he said he saw no reason why a hospital in India couldn't be as good as any in the world. 'My father says advanced medical facilities should be affordable; otherwise, it [the hospital] is elitist. So that's exactly what we are trying to do here,' he said.

We had heard of the concept of integrated and centralized healthcare, and it was at the Naik Healthcare Complex that we saw it in action. Located forty-five kilometres from Surat airport, on the Mumbai–Delhi National Highway, the complex is spread across eight acres and houses the cancer and multispecialty hospitals, accommodation for doctors and nursing staff, and a residential section for associated staff. Everything is within reach and easily accessible.

When you offer comprehensive care, you need facilities to match. The state-of-the-art facilities at Nirali Cancer Hospital include an advanced diagnostic centre, laboratories and facilities such as radiation oncology, linear accelerator, brachytherapy, advanced imaging systems and medical as well as surgical oncology. The hospital conducts an impressive number of surgeries and procedures, radiations and chemotherapy sessions every year. But above and beyond all lie the immeasurable aspect of trust. It has won the trust of thousands in south Gujarat and beyond. At Nirali hospital, they know they are in good hands. The hospital is part of India's National Cancer Grid.

We saw the clear stamp of Naik's charitable orientation all over—the fee structure is calibrated to the income level of the patient. Those who are relatively well-off pay the normal fee, while the economically disadvantaged pay what they can afford. But whatever you pay, the medical services that you get are the same.

Day-to-day operations of both hospitals have been assigned to the Apollo Group—one of the country's foremost hospital conglomerates. As a result of this association, Naik and the founder-director of the Apollo Group, Dr Prathap C. Reddy, grew to become close friends over the years.

The doctors and medical staff go about their daily work as if charged with a mission. Everyone we met—from the trustees to the doctors and staff—was on the same page. All of this contributes in its own way to the positive vibe of the place, a vibe that helps to heal.

When a senior doctor gestured towards the facilities and said with pride, 'You will find a hospital like this in New York,' it's a familiar echo of Naik's oft-repeated dictum at L&T—when you make something, making it as good as any in India is not good enough; it has to be as good as the best in the world.

A bridge connects the cancer and multispecialty hospitals, and you can, if appropriately authorized, simply walk across. The latter is larger than the cancer hospital, with 450 beds and a long list of services including general medicine, general surgery, cardiology and cardiothoracic surgery.

Within the same campus are three tall towers that offer accommodation for nurses, and across a hedge are villas, where senior doctors stay. Once again, it is Naik's 'walk-to-work' concept in action. As we wound our way back to the gate, we noticed, in one corner of the campus, a small marble temple. The Hindu god Shiva's mount, Nandi the bull, sits at the front of this little island of calm, which is frequented by patients' attendants wishing for a little extra help for the healing hands inside.

---

The healthcare complex in Navsari is obviously the proud flagship of Naik's healthcare initiatives. It is also the latest in the long list of medical centres set up by Naik, of which the first was the Kharel General Hospital. If you go to Kharel soon after visiting the Nirali Hospitals, the general hospital will certainly appear modest in scale. But it is the only hospital of its kind in the little town, and an obvious boon to all those who are not in a position to seek support in Surat, more than an hour's drive away.

But Kharel General Hospital also has something special—a residential facility for doctors and paramedical staff just a couple of minutes away. It is called Geetagram, after Naik's wife. With its placid set of independent bungalows under the shade of sal trees, it has the air of a rural retreat. Here again, it is the familiar walk-to-work concept, which serves a vital purpose.

For doctors who are prepared to relocate from city to village, one of the problems is accommodation. Where would they find a house as comfortable as the ones they are used to in cities? At Geetagram, the accommodation almost certainly offers greener environs and more tranquility than a noisy, clamorous city.

Another healthcare unit built by Naik is the Nirali Radiation Centre in Surat. It is also equipped with advanced facilities and offers the high standard of service that has come to be expected from the Trusts. This centre's staff goes out of its way to arrange accommodation in Surat for the families of patients from outside the city.

## Bringing best-in-class care

Naik says that if Gujarat is his Janmabhoomi, Mumbai is his Karmabhoomi. In Mumbai, we travelled to the central suburb of Powai to visit the Nirali–A.M. Naik Charitable Healthcare Facility.

Powai is a suburb of stark demographic contrasts—numerous high-rises imperiously distancing themselves from all who walk the earth, and under their shadow, a sprawl of shanties where zinc sheets serve as roofs and blue tarpaulins provide cover during the monsoons.

People from both these groups come to the facility because word has spread about its advanced facilities and capable team of doctors. So, whom does the facility focus its attention on?

Dr K.J. Kamat served as its chief medical officer until recently. He is also the personal physician to A.M. Naik, and in that capacity has a tough job on his hands because Naik is best described as an 'impatient patient, who flouts all professional medical advice'.

But ask Dr Kamat about the Powai facility and the people who genuinely qualify for its subsidized medical services and his answer is clear. 'This facility is in line with the philanthropic vision of Mr Naik. So we are primarily here to serve the disadvantaged. We are here to give the poor the kind of facilities they would never be able to experience elsewhere. But we can obviously not turn back anyone who has landed at our door. So even when we find a patient stepping out of the latest model Mercedes-Benz, they are welcome. The only thing we expect is that they do not claim the subsidies we offer the poor. I have told Mr Naik about this, and he is totally in agreement,' Dr Kamat said.

Regardless of income level and social stature, the quality services on offer at this day-care facility include three operation theatres, ophthalmology, dialysis, pathological and investigative diagnostics, and a sonography system that could rank among the best in the advanced healthcare sector. The facility has a footfall of 400 a day, and the numbers keep growing.

'We are on our toes all the time,' said Dr Kamat, and as if on cue, he had to rush to attend to a patient who had just been brought in.

## Turning a page

Just a couple of hundred metres from the imposing glass-and-concrete A.M. Naik Tower on the arterial Jogeshwari-Vikhroli Link

## Giving Back, the Naik Way

Road in Powai stands another emblem of excellence in a field very distinct from industry—the A.M. Naik School.

It has been just over a year since it was set up, and the institution has already become one of the most sought-after in central Mumbai.

Recent years have seen an education boom in India fuelled by various factors. Back in the day, 'education' for the children of middle- and upper-middle-class parents meant enrolling their wards in a few elitist schools or in institutions set up by community trusts. Else, they could send their kids to the ubiquitous 'convents'—schools set up by various missionary orders. No doubt they rendered yeoman's service at a critical phase in the country's evolution, but times have changed, and private schools now seem to rule the roost. Changing times have brought in changing aspirations. Children today have wider horizons—they want to do more, become more, with their aggressively aspirational parents encouraging them every step of the way.

Schools catering to the requirements of the uber-rich have mushroomed in such large numbers and so rapidly that they have become a kind of education factory, with nothing to distinguish one glitzy school from another.

It was in this competitive, sometimes corrosive environment that Naik thought of setting up his school. He had clear ideas about the kind of institution he wanted; it had to be a school grounded in the values he had espoused all his life—honesty, integrity, respect for elders and a deep, abiding love of your motherland.

In an address at the school, Naik talked at length about how his family had been connected to education. 'Education and community service have been part of my family tradition for three generations. My grandfather was the first principal of a traditional gurukul in south Gujarat,' he said.

In fact, there were so many teachers at his family home in Endhal, the villagers used to call it 'Master Kutumb' (the family of teachers). For the new school, Naik's objective was to 'equip children to become accomplished and proud citizens of modern India'.

The school's principal, faculty and even members of the support staff are all subjected to an interview by Naik. Every teacher has been hand-picked. On one memorable occasion, an interview was conducted while he was still convalescing, having summarily overruled the doctor's objections and rushed home from the hospital. Quite apart from appraising qualifications and experience, he has a way of gauging a person's intrinsic qualities. Do they have the fire inside? Can they be trusted? For answers, Naik goes by gut feel—that inexplicable but time-tested method of sizing up a person; his instincts have rarely let him down.

As we have seen across the book, every project for Naik begins with the selection of the leader—one who shares his vision and possesses the drive to turn plans on paper into reality. Naik was right on target in the selection of the school's principal, Dr Madhura Phadke. A well-known educationist, she has headed a clutch of schools before taking up what she said was 'probably the biggest challenge of my career—measuring up to Mr Naik's exacting expectations'.

School principals we believed were aloof, stern and intimidating, but Dr Phadke was different; she was all smiles and grace. She proudly showed us the distinctive features of the school. Its positive vibes begin with the high central atrium—bright, airy and stretching

## Giving Back, the Naik Way

up through all six floors. If it was designed to inspire school children to reach for the skies, it certainly serves the purpose.

The classrooms too are bright, airy and inviting. 'We believe that students need to be in classrooms that inspire them. They need to be happy to be here and look forward to coming every day,' she said.

The school has its own anthem, and we listened to it at the end of a cultural function, when well over 100 students filled the auditorium with the rousing number. It is a multilingual composition, and we must say that, transcending language barriers, every child sang it with full-throated gusto!

Speaking about the role that Naik shaped for her and other teachers, Dr Phadke gave us an insight into his character.

'The child in him is alive. He engages himself in everything connected with the school—from the logo to the teachers we recruit. When he visits the school, he insists on walking down the corridors and seeing things for himself,' she said.

Apparently, Dr Kamat, whom we met earlier, was not amused by this insistence. He asked Dr Phadke, 'Why are you making him walk so much'? She replied, 'What can I do? What can anyone do! Mr Naik says the school and all the children give him an energy charge.'

The A.M. Naik School had a VVIP inauguration; it was formally declared open by India's home minister, Amit Shah. Appropriately, the inauguration took place on Teachers' Day 2022, marking the birth anniversary of Sarvepalli Radhakrishnan, the teacher, philosopher and statesman who was India's second President.

Shah congratulated the school's founder on its stated aim of propagating intrinsically Indian values and added that India's New

Education Policy (NEP) drew on the principles which had been outlined by Radhakrishnan. In response, Naik mentioned that the school curriculum had indeed been aligned to the NEP.

Apart from the principal and the faculty and staff, Naik also selected K. Ramakrishnan, his former colleague from L&T, as a member of the school management committee. He, among others, helps to turn Naik's all-encompassing vision into brick and mortar. His work includes interfacing with the civic authorities, officials of different stripes and members of the board of education. Dealing with officialdom can never be easy, but Ram's zeal is unflagging and he is charged about his purpose. 'We are working not for a company but for a cause,' he said.

As we prepared to leave, we spotted high-spirited children striding down the corridor towards the school's music studios. 'They are in a hurry,' said Ram, 'to become tomorrow's Kishore Kumars and Latas!' Yes, the A.M. Naik School has studios for music, dance, art and craft. The aim, we reminded ourselves, is to produce well-rounded, not just well-read, citizens who will measure up to the school's motto: 'Learn, Lead, Achieve'.

**Bringing world-class education to rural Gujarat**

The eponymous school in Mumbai is the newest of a clutch of educational institutions that A.M. Naik has helped build over the years. Most of them are located in south Gujarat. In fact, when we drove along the Kharel stretch of NH 48, we found impressive evidence of Naik's philanthropy for over 500 metres on both sides of the road.

## Giving Back, the Naik Way

On one side stood a higher secondary school with hostels within the campus for girls and boys. Following that was the Anil Naik Technical Training Centre, with its own set of hostels. On the other side of the road, we came upon a primary school and a secondary school.

All of them stood out for some common features—they looked like they were built by one obsessed with detail. Every tile had to be in place, the landscaping done and the flowers ready to bloom. These are the exacting conditions that Naik used to impose on buildings in L&T's campus that were ready for inauguration. Else, he would simply not attend. Tough, yes, but that is how you elevate standards and that is how you build tomorrow.

The hostels for girls and boys located within the campus overcome a major problem that rural schoolchildren face—lack of accommodation. The facility is free, with only nominal charges being levied for boarding.

The whole enclave is often referred to as the A.M. Naik Education and Skilling Centre of Excellence. At the far end of the campus is a training centre for technical skills.

## Anil Naik Technical Training Centre

'A skill learnt,' says Naik, 'is a life transformed.' The Anil Naik Technical Training Centre is unique. It is the only institution of its kind in south Gujarat, specifically meant for school dropouts. As a smartly worded promotional pamphlet reads: 'The only qualification a candidate needs is … no qualification.'

You can look upon the place, then, as a centre not just to impart skills but also to mould lives. 'By imparting skills to dropouts,' said Naik, 'I am restoring the self-respect of young men and women. They begin to realize that they are worth something.' Skilling is especially useful for women, because it counters traditional gender biases and gives women a degree of financial independence. It should warm everyone's hearts to know that gender differentiation has been erased at ANTTC. While visiting the centre, we realized that a girl now has as much chance as a boy of becoming an electrician, solar power technician, welder or fitter. Bye-bye, bias!

Naik sees it as his personal mission to eradicate all the barriers that stand in the way of women empowerment. Never one for half measures, he gives us the details—girls of a certain age tend to drop out from school when they find a lack of toilets and adequate sanitary facilities. Naik made sure that toilets come up along with the schools that he has built and adopted.

Helping young men and women put their lives back on track at ANTTC is young Sneha Raut. She is the daughter-in-law of Priti Raut, Naik's niece, whom we met in the previous chapter.

Sneha tells us that she saw Naik as a kind and wise leader telling her about things that proved to be very valuable to her as a person and a professional.

At work in the training centre, Sneha is outspoken and unafraid. 'I am a fighter,' she said. Most of the fights she has had are with indolent students. 'Most of those who come here are self-motivated. But there are a few who need a nudge to make them motivated.'

## Giving Back, the Naik Way

Sneha is tackling a problem that many social workers have previously encountered—the inconvenient truth is that there will always be some youngsters unwilling to change. But Sneha is not one to be easily deterred. After all, she has learnt a thing or two from Naik!

The centre has secured recognition from the National Skill Development Corporation and runs classes for a broad spectrum of technical trades, including those for electricians, fitters, welders, etc. It has a placement rate of over 70 per cent. The institute's chief executive Winny Rawal, Sneha and the team keep monitoring feedback on training sessions and keep pace with the needs of a changing market. A couple of years ago, for instance, they decided to introduce a course for computer assistants which proved to be very popular.

Every hall that we visited was abuzz with activity—eager young boys and girls learning skills under the watchful eyes of experienced supervisors. They were poised on the cusp of transformation.

The Anil Naik Technical Training Centre is built on the pillars of hope, opportunity and aspiration. This world of ours cannot only be about winners; it must also be about those who tried but failed—this institution extends help to those who could not successfully complete their studies. It's here that a programme which was initiated by the NGO Pratham comes in. It is helping students complete their secondary education. ANTTC is partnering with Pratham in the endeavour, appropriately christened Second Chance.

As we drove away from the centre, we couldn't help musing on life, its uncertainties and its ups and downs. Don't we all need a second chance?

# A.M. Naik

## A 'Vaidik' school

Another school, and a very different one, with which Naik has been closely associated is in Magod, on the outskirts of Valsad. Everything about this school sets it apart—its curriculum, its faculty, its students and, most of all, its medium of instruction.

In this school, all lessons are taught in Sanskrit, the language hailed in Hindu tradition as belonging to the gods.

It was Naik's father-in-law, Dolatbhai Desai, who first told him about this unique institution in south Gujarat, modelled on the ancient gurukul system of learning. Naik's curiosity was piqued. An ashram for schoolgoing children in this day and age? What would they do in the future?

As he always does when his interest is aroused, Naik sought more information and discovered a different world—one where India's hallowed traditions shake hands with tomorrow.

The school has been set up by Shri Nityaananda, a disciple of the older Swami Muktananda. It is described as a confluence of 'Vedic knowledge and science'. The more Naik discovered about it, the more impressed he was—here was an institution that seemed to answer the need of the times. Education based on Western concepts of learning had its benefits but also its downside—it gave short shrift to native, intrinsic Indian values. Students graduating from mainstream schools emerged as cultural orphans, with little knowledge of their roots. Nothing was said explicitly, but it still led to the feeling among students that the only things worth respecting came from the West. This flew against Naik's own vision—he felt it was time Indian culture

## Giving Back, the Naik Way

was restored to a position of pride. 'If we Indians don't feel proud of our cultural heritage, who will?' he said.

The Naik Charitable Trust gave the school a large, new campus, named Geeta Vaidik Gram, after Mrs Naik. The campus, located within the Shanti Mandir ashram, includes hostels for the students, called chhatras (Sanskrit for students), and for the faculty 'acharyas'.

Naik suggested we visit Geeta Vaidik Gram, assuring us that it would be a kind of cultural awakening for us, set in our Western mores. It turned out to be more than a cultural wake-up call; it brought us in touch with our own dimly remembered personal philosophies.

We reached the wooded ashram at dusk and walked to the central hall. The atmosphere seemed so serene that we almost felt like alien intruders. The chhatras and the acharyas were performing sandhyavandanam, a sacred Vedic ritual. For an hour after that, the ashram was filled with mesmeric, melodious chants. The ritual is usually followed by a pravachan, or discourse, and then dinner, again in the open dining area. The day comes to an end post an hour-long self-study, or swadhyaya, session, during which students reflect on the day's teachings and prepare for school the next day.

Naik's office had phoned ahead and told the ashram to expect us, so we gained quick access to Swami Nityaananda, who presides over the institute. He has a calm, benign air about him—a person so obviously at peace with himself that he can transmit it to those who meet him. As we approached the saffron-robed Swamiji, we debated whether to address him in Hindi or ask for an interpreter, but we didn't need to—he welcomed us in English, his drawl carrying an accent much more refined than ours.

Unsurprisingly, in Swami Nityananda we found another fan of A.M. Naik. He has had a long association with Naik, which began with Dolatbhai Desai, Geetaben's father. The swami said Naik's way of philanthropy doesn't carry the attitude of a 'donor' but that of a genuine well-wisher. 'Mr Naik doesn't simply hand over a cheque and tell himself "My job is done",' he said.

The job is not done until the system delivers and the benefits become tangible. So Naik immerses himself in everything that he sets out to do. That is the attitude of a project manager.

Later, we accepted Swamiji's invitation to walk around the campus and see things for ourselves. 'You will see how a mindset oriented towards the West is turning towards India's heritage. You may even hear our students conversing with each other in Sanskrit,' he added.

By the end of the trip, we were more than hopeful that a language that seemed to be on the decline owing to ignorance and a warped sense of priorities would one day regain its lost glory.

---

In addition to the two trusts, the Nirali Memorial Medical Trust and the Naik Charitable Trust, a third—L&T Public Charitable Trust (LTPCT)—also chips in.

This trust has an unusual history—it was formed in 2004 as part of Naik's effort to propagate philanthropy. There appears to be a critical need for this. By and large, Indians do not score high on philanthropy and we are not known as a nation of givers. As chairman of LTPCT, Naik is doing his bit to change that. He believes every employee of L&T, if given the opportunity, could evolve into a high-impact change agent and contribute towards social development. As Gayatri Oleti, head of L&T Public Charitable Trust, said with visible delight: 'We are not a cost centre; we are a pride centre.'

Set up long before CSR spends became virtually mandatory for profit-making corporates, the composition and character of the LTPCT made it special—it belongs to the people of L&T as much as to the company because it is funded by employee contributions, with a matching grant by the company.

Beginning with a substantial contribution by employees, who were given employee stock options (ESOPs), and a matching grant given by L&T, LTPCT has grown consistently. That is how Naik had always wanted it—ESOPs had made employees financially secure, and he said it would be appropriate for the newfound wealth to be shared with the disadvantaged.

He has brought in professionals with the high energy levels required to keep the trust ticking. Gayatri Oleti had has a track record studded with accomplishments in community service across the country. Sensing that the intensity of her commitment matched her capabilities, Naik persuaded her to leave her position at a multinational and join the trust. Along with her team, she is one of the implementers of Naik's and the trust's vision across the sectors of healthcare, education, skill-building, water and sanitation, and livelihood.

The LTPCT has a part to play in all the initiatives in Kharel—the schools, the hostels and the skill training centre, ANTTC. The overarching emphasis now is on the tribal districts of Talasari, Vikramgarh (Maharashtra) and Dang (Gujarat). The trust's budget is large, but as Oleti says, it is never enough. There is always so much more to be done.

**Brand Naik in philanthropy**

Former cabinet secretary S. Rajgopal had told us: 'Naik does not only change the lives of individuals; he changes the face of the community around him. He has served L&T enough; now he wants to serve the country—a bigger vision.'

A common feature among the various philanthropic initiatives of Naik—except for the cancer hospitals built in memory of his late granddaughter, the trusts conducting and managing all philanthropic activities carry either Naik's full name or his surname. But this is not just for publicity. Naik has achieved so much in his lifetime that he is a brand unto himself. So publicity is perhaps the last thing he craves.

What, then, is the motive behind the names? We believe it is a deliberate move—Naik is putting his reputation on the line, his brand value at stake. He wants to ensure that the institutions he is building live up to the qualities he himself is synonymous with—trust, reliability and best-in-class delivery.

Naik is also doing his bit to propagate the idea of philanthropy among all those he is in touch with. At speeches, seminars and conferences, a recurring theme is that community service needs more willing hands. Perhaps the most important thing that he has done is having pulled down the silken barriers to philanthropy, making it accessible to all. It is not a preserve of the wealthy, he seems to say. With a little effort, we can all discover the philanthropist in ourselves.

## Giving Back, the Naik Way

In November 2023, when Hurun India's announcement reaffirmed Naik's position as India's most generous professional business leader, he sent a note to all in the company, urging them to 'integrate philanthropy into everyday lives'. The letter made a fervent appeal to be more generous and forthcoming.

'Helping others is uniquely soul-satisfying,' Naik said. 'The happiness you will feel from seeing the smiles on the faces of disadvantaged children relieved of pain and hunger is indescribable—something money cannot buy.'

When asked what he thought of the work he has done, Naik is candid: 'One life is too short a time to do so many things. Mentally, I am still in my forties, but this body has aged twice as fast and prevents me from doing more. These initiatives are all very close to my heart, and I would have loved to devote more time and energy to them. I have created the concepts, put in place the systems and processes, and recruited the right people for the right jobs. I have set the ball rolling. Now it is up to the next generation to carry forward the torch. I am confident that they will do a good job.'

---

It is sometimes assumed that philanthropy is an activity conducted at a benign pace with no urgent agenda or deadlines bearing down upon you. It is something that you can do, for instance, on slow Saturday afternoons. Naik is emphatic proof that genuine, heartfelt philanthropy is nothing of the kind. His niece Priti corroborates this. 'Earlier, he used to tell me that one should account for every minute that you spend. Now, he says that every second is important.

Even in the case of philanthropy, he does it with a professional approach,' she said.

Naik has groomed a group of meticulous multi-taskers, adept at doing many things in parallel. Site visits, meetings with senior government officials plus the occasional function to foster esprit de corps—it's all part of the job.

With the help of the younger generation in the family, Naik's philanthropy is sharply focused, with measurable targets and candid appraisals to ensure that everything is on track. He proves that you can be large-hearted about community service but also hard-nosed. Every rupee you spend on the community must be counted, its outcome measured. Has your money achieved what it was intended to accomplish? It Is comparable to other similar activities? Or could more have been achieved with less?

Like everything else that Naik has embarked upon through his life, philanthropy too is a demanding activity that can stretch your physical and mental abilities. And there are no full stops—at least in Naik's case.

Months ago, he had said that once he had got the hospitals, schools and the skill training centre going, there would be nothing more to be done. But just the other day, we heard him talking about acquiring a new plot adjacent to the ANTTC in Kharel.

'It's on the other side of the nullah,' he said, bubbling with excitement like a research scientist who had made an unexpected discovery. 'It will help us expand the hostel for the training centre. Imagine! We can help so many more young boys and girls.'

His enthusiasm for doing something new, something more, is inexhaustible. This man, we told ourselves, is never going to say,

## Giving Back, the Naik Way

'Bas! I can't do any more'. Stray lines from wisdom literature of another age come to mind: 'Those who reach the inn and call it quits are missing the whole point of life. For in reality, there is no inn. It is the road, now and forever.'

And as you read this, Mr Naik is back on the road, set to expand the ANTTC on the adjacent plot of land, which he recently bought, to train more school dropouts and widen the spectrum of the trades at the existing training centre. Along with the expanded skill training facility will come up an institute to 'train the trainers'. As we have seen, this model has worked successfully on Madh Island in Mumbai and Naik wants to replicate it in Kharel. Will there be an adequate number of trainers who seek further training in rural Gujarat? Some say that it is not going to work, but Naik has repeatedly proved that he can do what most people dismiss as impossible. And whatever he does, you can be sure, will be world class. As he said, 'The poor should not be told to make do with poor service.' On such robust optimism are tomorrows built.

---

Naik never sees the end of the road. He just goes on and on. He enjoys giving—giving his time, his counsel, his energy and, most of all, himself. As H. Jackson Brown Jr said, 'The happiest people are not those getting more, but those giving more'.

On the kind of journey that A.M. Naik is undertaking, there can be no full stops, no final destination. There will be only milestones along the way.

# 12

## The Flag Flies High

*'L&T is a fantastic organization. I am sure it will touch greater and greater heights.'*

'MY LIFE IS L&T. MY LEGACY IS L&T ...' SAID NAIK, HIS baritone voice rolling through the cavernous Birla Matushree Hall in south Mumbai, holding his audience in thrall. Always a captivating speaker, Naik knew that the 78th AGM would call for a special piece of oratory. It was his 25th AGM since he took the helm of L&T and the last time that he would chair the meeting. He therefore took the occasion to look back on his life and career, and narrate the fascinating story of a journey studded with milestones. He had taken the company to heights it had never attained before. He had envisioned its path to the future and drawn up the blueprint for its growth. Most of all, he had fought for it. Two decades ago, when the company had found itself in a crisis that endangered its existence, it was Naik who had stood up and raised the banner of resistance. The architect of L&T was also its saviour.

Having brought the company back from the brink, Naik did not bask in the glow of his achievements. There were things to be attended to, important issues to be addressed, new heights to be touched. The setting up of an employee trust fund would go a long way in protecting L&T's unique professional character. But what about the issue of succession? Who would succeed him at the helm and ensure that his unique legacy would never lose its lustre? As he put it: 'Succession planning has really succeeded if I am forgotten. I want to be forgotten.' That is an outcome that is unlikely ever to happen, but we understood what he meant.

Succession at L&T, as with many large companies in the country, had always been fraught with uncertainty and riddled with questions like 'Is Mr X really cut out for this?' or 'Does Mr Y have the experience needed?' L&T was a large and complex conglomerate. Heading the ship and steering it successfully called for exceptional abilities and a deep, intimate understanding of what makes this company tick. It was this issue that Naik sought to address. Whatever he takes up, he does a thorough job of it—there are no half measures, any time, anywhere. So the question of selecting the next CEO was subjected to the full weight of Naik's keen analysis. An uncanny judge of character, he had to impartially weigh every candidate's strengths and shortcomings and study the pros and cons. Naik refused to be hurried into it. He knew of companies which had been affected by

## The Flag Flies High

ill-thought succession planning and he did not want it to happen to L&T ever. So he kept his eyes open and his mind ticking.

And then one day, at an airport project of L&T in Delhi, Naik came across a live wire. He was an engineer who seemed to be able to grasp issues quickly and comprehensively, he could express his thoughts well, and he had an impressive career record in L&T. Could he finally be the person Naik was looking for? It would have been premature to come to an immediate judgement, and there were many pros and cons that needed to be weighed. But Naik kept him in mind. His name: S.N. Subrahmanyan.

---

Fast forward to an enlightening moment when we managed to interview Subrahmanyan, newly appointed as L&T's chairman and managing director. You would have come across his quotes frequently in this book, as he offered distinctive perspectives that helped us build a word-picture of Naik's capabilities, character and style. These happened on the fly, and we dutifully took notes. But we could not buttonhole him for any length of time.

Finally, one day, we managed to grab half an hour from his frenetic schedule at his modestly appointed cabin in Landmark, Andheri. Subrahmanyan spoke warmly and at length about his illustrious predecessor.

Subrahmanyan exudes a quiet sense of authority that is sometimes broken with an almost boyish smile, like the sun breaking through a cloud bank. He smiled as he reminisced about his many and varied interactions with Naik and recalled the many lessons he has learnt.

We asked SNS the million-dollar question, the answer to which the whole world would want to know: 'What are your feelings on taking on the mantle?' We received an answer that had a mix of humility, practical reality and, at the end, a bit of poetry.

'These are big shoes to fill, and I have small feet. As I told you, it's not my intention to fill his shoes. It cannot be done. People like Mr Naik come once in a few generations. So what I do is I take some things that I have learnt from him—some principles—and repeat the formula while taking the company forward,' he said.

Subrahmanyan is a true-blue L&T man, and identifies with the organization. 'People are empowered,' he said. 'We all feel like owners. You feel that this is your company ... and if anything happens to it, you feel hurt. If something good happens, you feel good. It has become part of your life.'

This is the kind of emotional ownership that Naik helped foster among all employees. It is also built in large measure by the participative nature in which L&T works.

'The bosses give you freedom to take decisions; it's not all top-down,' said SNS.

The ties that bind employees to the organization are almost familial. It is said that you may leave L&T if you choose, but L&T will not leave you. An enabling environment that prompted the young engineering graduate to hold fast to the organization and rise from graduate engineer trainee to chairman and managing director. After Naik, he is the best illustration of how the high road of opportunity is open to all at L&T. Talent comes out on top.

## The Flag Flies High

In an interview with *Fortune India*, Subrahmanyan had said with characteristic self-deprecation, 'I am a boring CEO (actually he is chairman and managing director) of a boring company.' It was a typical LOL moment. Everyone knew it wasn't true. Subrahmanyan can, when he chooses, make sparkling company. As for L&T, it simply cannot be boring; it is buzzing. We recall seeing a vintage advertisement released decades ago, featuring the famed L&T monogram under the headline: 'Nothing stays static behind this symbol'. If that was so true decades ago, it is even more true now.

Change has been ingrained into L&T's DNA. This company seems to have honed the technique of achieving a fine balance between spectacular change and sedate continuity. Its portfolio of businesses keeps pace with the market, and yet the company remains anchored to its traditional ethos. As a senior executive explained: 'It's the difference between "what" and "why". What we make or do keeps changing; why we do it has been constant for as long as I can remember.'

---

What exactly is the 'L&T culture' which A.M. Naik had guarded so zealously, and of which S.N. Subrahmanyan will be the new custodian and keeper of the flame?

Now, culture has always been hard to pin down in words and so the L&T culture was known more by through illustrative examples rather than precise definition. But as we pored through the company's archives, we came across an approximate answer to the question of culture. It was couched in an address that the company's high-profile HR head once delivered to youngsters who had recently joined the company. We carry a few excerpts of special relevance:

## People

L&T is ultimately its people—people like you [he is addressing young employees]. You are the ones who shape our character and script our success stories. You will also get a sense of the importance we give to people by just looking at the name of our company. Back in the day, our founders could have called the company anything that came to mind. They could have used fancy adjectives or coined a new word. But the two Danish engineers asked themselves—who are the doers, who is behind all this? It's us. Since then, it has been people all the way. The company that bears the names of two people—Henning Holck-Larsen and Søren Kristian Toubro—is now in the hands of all of you.

## Care and trust

A key word in the Vision Statement that was formulated soon after Mr A.M. Naik took over as CEO is 'trust'. Trust cannot be bought or supplied. You need to *earn* it; build the trust of the people you interact with. One of the ways you win trust is by caring. We have a tradition of caring for our own people, for our customers for the community around us and in a larger perspective, for the country we belong to. That is because we are not here for the short term; the relationships we build with our customers and all our constituents is for the long haul. We enjoy a continuing, long-term relationship with our major customers. Take ONGC, NTPC, Reliance, government bodies. We have worked towards earning their trust and retaining it.

## Continuous learning

Your first question could well be—why learn? Don't we know a lot already, and can't we just learn on the job? The answer is—not if you are an L&T-ite. We are a learning organization and will continue to be one. That does not mean that we are starting off ignorant but that we are keen to know more, dive deeper and expand our frontiers. And we keep alive that zeal. Let's not forget, the world is not standing still. The subjects we have spent years learning can rapidly morph into something with which we are no longer familiar. Training helps us keep abreast of developments in a fast-paced world.

At L&T, we don't just encourage learning, we induct it into our calendar. Most importantly, we invest in it—through our people and our facilities. Our training umbrella covers everyone—from youngsters like you right up to the those who have put in decades of experience. In fact, back in the late 1950s, we were one of the first companies in India to have in place an Apprentice Training Scheme.

Few companies in the country have as many and as well-equipped training institutions as we do. Many of you will soon see our Leadership Development Academy at Lonavala, a hill station a little over 80 km from here (Powai, Mumbai).

# A.M. Naik

## Innovation and entrepreneurship

Innovation is finding the pearl in the oyster of opportunity. We have a string of pearls. You know that L&T started in 1938 by importing Danish equipment. A year later World War II broke out, and the German naval blockade of Europe meant that our trade line was choked. So what did the partners do? They could well have stood aside and waited patiently till the conflict was over, but they were active and innovative rather than passive and reactive. So, they simply decided to manufacture what they earlier imported. That is one form of innovation!

You can innovate in making a product or you can innovate in the process. Let me give examples of process innovation first: an innovative form of welding called 'Trijunction welding' helped us build critical equipment for nuclear reactors. Since those early days, we have gone miles further in welding technology, but I am harking back to tri-junction welding because it was a milestone in our quest to learn and keep learning. There are similar examples that can be drawn from each of our businesses.

All our equipment which were 'Made in India' and set a precedent for Indian industry involved innovation at some stage of manufacture. There are plenty of examples: India's first indigenous hydrocracker reactor, first ethylene oxide reactor, world's biggest FCC regenerator and the sequence of superlatives which describe our achievements in construction—'biggest', 'tallest', 'fastest' ....

There are no full stops in an innovator's mind. One successful innovation clears the pathway for another, and yet another.

# The Flag Flies High

## Integrity

Integrity is a single word with multiple layers of meaning. It means honesty, and the commitment you make to yourself to navigate life using a moral compass. Let me take a leaf from our history book. Once, an ambitious young sales engineer managed to clinch a sale by overstating the features of his product. When the company's co-founder Soren Toubro heard of this, he was not impressed. He told the engineer: 'Young man, you have sold a product you do not have. That doesn't count for anything.' The message was clear—to the engineer concerned, and to succeeding generations. And the message was simple: truth is the best salesman.

Often, it can be hard to maintain integrity. It will seem much easier to take shortcuts. But in the long run, integrity pays off in the image you create and the reputation you enjoy. Now fast forward by a few decades. In the late 70s and 80s, India was going through a cement famine. Unscrupulous manufacturers jumped into the fray to exploit the situation and make a quick buck by adulterating the product, and selling short—meaning that the cement bags would be marked 50 kg but the factories would put in only 45 kg. It was at that time that a senior government representative requested L&T to get into cement manufacture. It was not only because they wanted an additional manufacture in the market but, more importantly, they wanted an honest manufacturer—a manufacturer for whom 50 kg meant 50 kg. In other words, when the Government of India wanted a company with integrity, they chose L&T.

## Customer focus

We have always been a customer-centric company. Our very first tagline used to be 'In Service Lies Success' ... it set the tone for our orientation towards business. We are here because of our customers ... Our relationship with our customers does not end with a sale. That's only one milestone on a long road. We stay in touch with the customer to enquire about performance and maintenance, and make sure that the product we have sold is delivering the value we had claimed. Such gestures do not remain a secret because word spreads. L&T became known to be different and we took the first steps on the path to growth and glory.

## Quality and safety

Our reputation for quality is widely known. The general feeling is that if it is L&T, it must be good. This is not being said by us but by our customers. Real estate companies used to promote their projects by stating in their ads 'Construction by L&T'. They were selling their buildings by riding the L&T brand. We put a stop to this later because we found it was being misused.

## Corporate social responsibility

In 2008, when Mr Naik released L&T's first sustainability report, L&T became the first company in the EPC space in India to disclose our performance across the traditional 3Ps—planet, people, profits. Since then, we have rigorously maintained our reporting cycle. And what did our first sustainability report say? It said that for L&T, CSR is nothing new. In fact, we were practising social responsibility even before the term came into vogue. Our factories and their surroundings used to be green, we would take care to minimize pollution and we set up medical clinics to provide assistance to members of the community. We did all this—not because we wanted to be good corporate citizens or because we wanted to get it published in our CSR reports. We did it simply because it was a natural part of who we are. In other words, we internalized the principles of CSR.

## Builders to the nation

Mr A.M. Naik joined the company over fifty years ago. He says that as a young man, fresh out of engineering college, there were only two criteria he had for a dream career destination, viz., it should be an engineering company, and second, it should contribute to nation-building. So, L&T was an obvious choice. That is why even though there was a hiccup at the interview stage, Mr Naik was clear. He said that it was 'my dream to join L&T, and so I am joining any way'.

All that I have just said, are strands that make up the grand tapestry of the L&T culture. Let me add that it is more lyrically expressed in our anthem. It begins with the lines: *'Jiski mitti se paida huay hum, karz hum us zameen ka chukaye'* (We must redeem the debt we owe to the land we are born in). You will be hearing our anthem many times. Pay attention to the words and the visuals. That's L&T in a nutshell.

# A.M. Naik

We were at the final stages of this book when we heard happy news. L&T had been certified as a Great Place to Work. The certification comes from an organization whose altruistic mission is to help improve workplace culture, and the award seems to count for a lot across industry. It is apparently recognized around the world, and is supposed to be considered by employees and employers as a high watermark in identifying excellent workplace cultures. It meant that L&T excelled on the dimensions of trust, high performance culture, credibility, respect, fairness, pride and camaraderie.

But, frankly, we were not surprised. All through the course of researching for and writing this book, the overwhelming impression we got was of a happy company. In our interactions with L&T employees across hierarchies and geographies, we sensed an unspoken but irrepressible regard for the organization, and a visible feeling of pride in belonging to it. Within themselves, they would joke about their salaries, and moan the long hours at work but it was all good-natured banter. In their hearts, they knew that with L&T, they were in good hands.

We did hear occasional murmurs of discontent in some quarters, but it was obvious that they came from congenital complainers who are an inescapable part of every company. The overall mood was in sync with what we had heard from both Naik and Subrahmanyan—'this is a fantastic company'. It echoed what Naik had told us when he talked of the company uniting against predators. 'What outsiders don't realize is that the people of L&T love L&T. No matter what, they will never be disloyal.'

# The Flag Flies High

## Transition: The L&T way

Countries have flags; companies usually don't. But L&T is not your usual company. In July 2023, when Naik suggested that L&T have a specially designed flag, the idea found ready acceptance. The newly designed flag had elements that were already accepted around the company as among the elements that make up the L&T mystique—the specific shade of yellow and the time-honoured, iconic monogram. Put together, they make up what has been gushingly referred to as a 'fabric of fervour'. Naik has had a lot to do with helping the flag fly high.

In fact, decades ago, when L&T's newly formed IT company was debating its logo, opinion was sharply divided. Professional design consultants were brought in, including one of the country's largest brand-identity designers. Old timers recall that the agency recommended that the company monogram be dispensed with because it was too closely associated with an old company and, therefore, 'lacked a contemporary touch'.

Overawed and perhaps intimidated by the design firm's credentials, most of the company executives were prepared to go along with the recommendations made by the firm. Only Naik stood in opposition. He said a change of logo was unnecessary, wasteful and counterproductive. It may please the vanity of the design firm (bagging the L&T account would rank as a coup in agency circles), but it would be detrimental to the company's interests. He recollected the number of times business prospects had told him how they recalled the logo and how it touched a chord among Indians, at home and abroad. Piling fact on fact, he skilfully made a case for leaving the logo intact and then, with rhetorical flourish, turned to the much decorated brand expert to ask: 'Now, you tell me exactly what we will gain by changing our logo.' Game over. The logo has stayed exactly as it always was.

Company bards have waxed lyrical about its monogram, saying it flutters at distant heights, it has soared into outer space, it has travelled around the world. Yet, it stays embedded in every heart. The grand cavalcade had begun with the legendary founders, Henning Holck-Larsen and Søren Kristian Toubro, and then a succession of distinguished leaders. The leader who took the flag to the greatest heights is undoubtedly A.M. Naik.

It was this badge of honour and repository of collective pride that Naik would be handing over to Subrahmanyan, at functions in four major L&T locations held in the months preceding 30 September 2023. All of them served a single purpose—communicating with clarity that a major transition was taking place.

Naik spoke at length at each of the functions. Discarding his prepared text, he went on a rambling but riveting account of his association with L&T. The event was a long river of nostalgia that began with the day he first walked through the gates of L&T.

The message was clear: the legacy of L&T needs to be taken forward, with all its values and ethos intact.

But it was not all rose-tinted nostalgia; it served a purpose—to highlight seamless transition. This is, unfortunately, a rarity in the country today. Industry is rife with examples of hastily drawn succession plans going awry. Succession often descends into a messy, unpleasant affair. The causes vary—from sibling rivalry to personal incompatibility. The waters are muddied with claims and counterclaims. All this leads to much bitterness and recrimination.

## The Flag Flies High

In an era when succession issues in closely held family businesses often become complex, hitting the streets and courts, the succession plan Naik devised for L&T went off exactly as planned. Speaking at the flag handing over function in Chennai, S. Gurumurthy put it more eloquently. He said, 'Naik handed over his entire power and responsibility to his successor with the smoothness that bettered the baton hand over at an Olympic relay race,' adding, 'It illustrated how different L&T was from other companies.'

Gurumurthy went on to say: 'I spoke to Mr Subrahmanyan and he told me that Naik had prepared a succession plan for him. Now I am thinking about my own succession plan. Who will take over from me? This is the remarkable thing about L&T—every leader thinks not about themselves, but about the team.'

Several of Naik's old colleagues spoke as well, offering their different perspectives. But all of them together made up a fascinating portrait of Naik, the leader.

Subrahmanyan rose to the occasion with a speech that was in equal measure about the honour and responsibility that he has taken up and about his deep gratitude to Naik for bringing the company to this exalted level.

Long-time colleagues say Naik had always been good at succession planning; even before he took over, he had been meticulous in planning the succession at levels far below the apex.

At every level, Naik would draw up a list of professionals best equipped to take over from him. Who was the best to head planning? Who could be a useful person at the head of stores? Who would head the assembly section? He knew the role and he knew his people, and he had no problem getting his opinion accepted.

Few people know as much about the workings of organization as Gurumurthy and we plied him for more information. Gurumurthy has had a ringside view of how several organizations have contended with the challenge of change at the helm. He told us: 'To create a succession plan under Indian conditions is not easy. Typically, there is destruction of company values and ethics, and little commitment to shareholders. That is not succession planning; that is recklessness. Naik showed professionalism in the way succession was aligned to consistency and continuity.'

He turned to us and asked a rhetorical question: 'Can you show me any other example in the corporate world? The fact is Naik is both L&T's child and L&T's father. All relationships are expressed there.' We left it at that, as the last word on the subject.

---

Naik is never overgenerous with praise; he probably believes it lulls the recipient into complacency—a throwback perhaps to his father, who would never give his son full marks even if all was correct. But Naik makes a few exceptions, and one of them is for Subrahmanyan. There is no way, he believes, that his successor could ever be complacent, so he is warm in praise and affection.

Wishing him on his birthday in 2023, Naik wrote:

> Dear SNS,
>
> A very happy birthday to you! May the Almighty continue to shower His blessings on you and your family, and keep you all in excellent health.

## The Flag Flies High

The youthful vigour with which you address each day and the passion you infuse into everything you do holds a shining light for the company. The positive impact of your work is helping to make a significant difference and, I am sure, it will continue to do so far into the future.

I am confident that you will triumph over every challenge in your path, help L&T soar to greater heights and keep its legacy shining bright.

What will the face of tomorrow's L&T look like? The business magazine *Fortune India* attempts an answer in its issue of April 2024. In it, Naik is quoted as saying: 'Though L&T might evolve further, it will not deviate much from the platforms already created for growth.' CMD Subrahmanyan agrees whole-heartedly. One of the chief platforms that Naik built in the early part of this century revolved around IT. It is Naik's IT vision which lit the way for a new and exciting chapter in the L&T story that Subrahmanyan is helping to script.

Subrahmanyan had his roots in the old economy, a true-blue infrastructure and construction professional. But he was good at reading the future, and his crystal ball would have told him that the future is digital. Other companies may have read the signs of the time too but L&T saw digital's panorama of possibilities a shade ahead of the rest of the pack, and has become the de facto flagbearer of 'digital construction'. New technologies have had a massive impact at every phase—right from conception stage to tendering to construction to O&M. Digitally powered project execution is almost a whole new ball game. It has become faster, safer, cleaner, more accurate, less polluting, economical, and most importantly, use of technology has shaped a more sustainable growth path for the company.

What began in a small way to explore how the computer could take the place of men in routine activities, soon assumed centre stage. The last six or seven years have seen spectacular advances, and remarkably, none of the technologies L&T put to use was bought off the shelf. They had been developed in-house—*'aatmanirbhar'* (self-reliance) in action!

Paradoxically, it was the pandemic which provided a boost. Necessity being the mother of invention, the COVID crisis created the urgency to get digital technologies implemented in 2021. During the pandemic, when the trend across industries and companies was to conserve cash and to opt for austerity measures, L&T invested heavily in digital technology and Industrial Internet of Things (IIoT) to automate its manufacturing processes.

Recalling the journey, Subrahmanyan is happy—but it is important to add—he is not complacent. He said: 'Construction was the area where I grew up and when I look back, I could implement one of the largest digital programmes anywhere in this space in the world.'

We asked about the kind of technologies that were at play in L&T's sites across the country and abroad. We were told it was the whole spectrum. There was AI, ML, AR, VR, Cloud, Big Data & Analytics, drones, GPS, RFID & QR Codes, LiDAR, BIM, IoT, 3D printing across all the verticals. Across all L&T's project sites and manufacturing bases, over 14,000 equipment and other assets are digitally connected. From these emerge rich data sets that

## The Flag Flies High

enable L&T to make extensive use of data analytics to optimize asset utilization and to plan resources and inventories better. Safety also gets a boost. Use of robotics has helped in making previously hazardous operations accident-free.

Even on the manufacturing front, adoption of smart technologies has propelled it up the value chain. We had touched on this briefly in the chapter on Hazira. The same qualitative changes are visible in all L&T facilities for aerospace, nuclear power and defence—sectors deeply entrenched with India's '*aatmanirbharta*' (self-reliance) aspirations.

Today you cannot talk of change in industry without bringing in climate change. As an industry bellwether, L&T is leading the way in fighting climate change and building a sustainable future. Its targets are clear: becoming Water Neutral by 2035 and becoming Carbon Neutral by 2040.

We gathered that depending on how the market opportunities unfold, the company would invest over the next 3–4 years up to USD 2–2.5 billion in the areas of green hydrogen, solar and wind projects. L&T has already begun manufacture of electrolysers and this is just the start. The plan is to manufacture and supply other critical components such for green hydrogen, storage batteries and fuel cells. To tap the opportunities and scale up faster, L&T has already forged strategic partnerships with both domestic and international players.

L&T's perspective planners and corporate strategists peering into their computers are upbeat and optimistic. They are confident that going forward, new tech will be the true enabler for India to consolidate its position as a driver of global growth. If this can happen successfully, and here we cross our fingers, India should be able to achieve 'developed country' status much ahead of our PM's target year of 2047.

And that's another story that time will tell.

---

The L&T flag flutters in L&T's campuses, in the offices of top executives and in major conference rooms. There, it stands alongside the national flag, and in deference, a few inches below it. This is a company with total clarity about the purpose of it all—it is engaged in building the nation.

After the last flag handover ceremony concluded at the plush Jio World Garden in BKC, Mumbai on 30 September 2023, and as Naik and his family were preparing to get back home, we asked him if he felt a twinge of regret on handing over control of the company that was, in many ways, his life. 'On the contrary, I am overjoyed,' Naik said. 'I actually enjoy the act of giving. I have realized the truth of what my father told me long ago: "Taking is a burden. Giving is a blessing."'

# Acknowledgements

*'Success blossoms from seeds of collaboration;*
*every hand that helps plant them*
*is part of the bloom.'*

MR A.M. NAIK IS AN INDELIBLE PART OF VERY MANY LIVES. OF the multitude who know him, we restricted ourselves to a little over sixty people from different vocations and geographies. Else, this book could become an anthology of opinion. Every one of those whom we met was unfailingly generous with their time, and opened for us a treasure trove of remembrances, information and insight. We thank them all.

We also thank those whose views may not have found mention here owing to the constraints of space and context. However, our

## Acknowledgements

thanks go out to each of them for the time they spent with us, and we appreciate their courtesy.

This book has an anchor: P.R. Kothari, an L&T veteran who has worked for decades directly under Mr Naik, and has his finger on the pulse of the large, complex and growing company. He played a major part in bringing together and directing the authors' efforts into a cogent story.

Mr Naik's extended family is blessed with infinite patience. We taxed this virtue to the fullest with our recurring queries and clarifications. Thank you, Mrs Geeta Naik, Jignesh and Rucha, Pratiksha and Mukul and Mr Naik's two vivacious grandchildren, Riya and Sharini. (Take a bow, Rucha, this book owes a lot to your marvellous eye for detail.) We thank Priti and Sneha for chipping in with invaluable help.

We requested several former directors (both executive and independent) and other senior executives of L&T to travel back in time—often multiple decades—to relive their old association with Mr Naik. They did so gladly and came up with priceless gems from the past. We acknowledge with gratitude their wisdom, candour and wit.

L&T's chairman and managing director, S.N. Subrahmanyan, and his colleagues on the executive committee rank among the busiest, charged as they are with the mission of taking the company to the next orbit of growth. Still they took time out from their busy schedules and provided distinctive facets of Mr Naik's personality that enabled us and our readers to see a 'once-in-a-generation' leader in action.

Acknowledgements

Finally, we thank Sumeet Chatterjee, head of L&T's Corporate Brand Management and Communications. We also owe a lot to Arijit Hajra—part of Sumeet's team. Allergic to limelight, he is the quintessential backroom asset whose contribution was invaluable. Mugdha Trivedi, executive assistant to Mr Naik, was tasked with interfacing between authors and respondents and performed an unobtrusive but effective balancing act among multiple offices.

We do hope that this book will make all their efforts worthwhile.

# About the Authors

**Priya Kumar** is the author of sixteen books and is a specialist in distilling the accomplishments of corporate figures, entrepreneurs and sports stars into inspirational biographies.

**Jairam N. Menon** is a versatile writer whose long experience of working at L&T, and in proximity to the corporate office, gave him a ringside view of A.M. Naik in action.

# HarperCollins *Publishers* India

At HarperCollins India, we believe in telling the best stories and finding the widest readership for our books in every format possible. We started publishing in 1992; a great deal has changed since then, but what has remained constant is the passion with which our authors write their books, the love with which readers receive them, and the sheer joy and excitement that we as publishers feel in being a part of the publishing process.

Over the years, we've had the pleasure of publishing some of the finest writing from the subcontinent and around the world, including several award-winning titles and some of the biggest bestsellers in India's publishing history. But nothing has meant more to us than the fact that millions of people have read the books we published, and that somewhere, a book of ours might have made a difference.

As we look to the future, we go back to that one word—a word which has been a driving force for us all these years.

Read.